S0-BSB-715

LEADERSHIP

THE POWER OF A CREATIVE LIFE

LEADERSHIP

THE POWER
OF A
CREATIVE LIFE

RICK JOYNER

MorningStar

P.O. Box 19409
Charlotte, NC 28219-9409

Leadership, The Power of a Creative Life
Copyright © 2001 by Rick Joyner

Distributed by MorningStar
P.O. Box 19409, Charlotte, NC 28219-9409

International Standard Book Number 1-929371-07-1

MorningStar's website: www. morningstarministries.org
For information call 704-522-8111.

No part of this book may be reproduced or transmitted in any form or by any means, electronic, mechanical, including photocopying, recording, or by any information storage and retrieval system, without written permission from the author.

Cover Photo by Daryl Benson/Masterfile
Cover Design by Micah Davis
Book Layout by Sharon Taylor

All rights reserved.
Printed in the United States of America.

TABLE OF CONTENTS

FOREWORD

L eadership and creativity are two of the most powerful forces on earth. Together they have dictated the course of history. They can be used for good or evil, creating a wide swath across the human landscape. This book is a study of these two forces, and how they can be developed in your life.

The seed for this book was actually another book that I wrote entitled *Leadership, Management, and the Five Essentials for Success.* To my surprise, that book quickly became our top bestseller. I determined then that if it was going to have the potential distribution for which it was obviously headed, it merited revision. This book contains everything in the original version rewritten for better organization and flow, along with a considerable amount of new material. It also contains some remarkable historic and contemporary examples of how the principles of this book have been applied with success.

This book is written in the simple, straightforward language of "the common man" (or woman). I did this because the greatest souls who have walked the earth, those who have risen to the highest levels of leadership and creativity, have almost always emerged from the midst of the common, the usual, and the ordinary. The key to releasing both of these powerful life forces is usually found in the midst of struggles, especially the struggle for identity, that are the common dreams of the common man and woman.

The only difference between *ordinary* and *extraordinary* is *extra.* The extra that is required to do this can be amazingly little. One small step can begin the breakthrough. Every common and ordinary life has the potential to be uncommon and extraordinary. This book is intended to give the encouragement and resolution to take the steps that lead to the fulfillment for which you were created.

One of the great philosophical questions is whether the times make the man, or the man makes the times. Was Napoleon a product of the times in which he lived, or did he make them what they were? Of course, there is some truth to both perspectives. History testifies very resoundingly that man makes his own way, but both leadership and creativity can be developed. Napoleon, and every other extraordinary leader in history, could have been lost in the shuffle of humanity if something had not been awakened in them.

This book addresses these two great forces of leadership and creativity together because they are not only related—they are inseparable. True leadership is impossible without creativity, and creativity is released through leadership. The more clearly we understand the link between these two the more readily they can be released in our lives. Even so, one can possess great creative leadership and be doomed to failure unless it is combined with the third great power that all lasting human achievement requires—effective management skills.

The primary goal of this book is to release the power of creative leadership in a way that will insure positive and lasting accomplishments through effective management. King Solomon, who is referred to in the Bible as the wisest man who had lived on the earth, wrote: "And if one can overpower him who is alone, two can resist him. A cord of three strands is not quickly torn apart." Leadership, creativity, and management are three characteristics that can form just such a cord. Standing alone, any one of these can be easily overcome. Properly joined together, they become a powerful and effective force that is nearly invincible.

You may rightly wonder what my credentials are for writing on these subjects. First, my life experiences are the foundation for what I have written. I was raised in conditions that would seemingly limit me to a life of mediocrity or failure, but through the application of these principles, I now have a track record of significant success. When my family disintegrated, my formal education stopped at the ninth grade. I have now written a number of best-selling books, some of which have been translated into nearly forty languages. I edit and write in a quarterly journal, which features articles that are being distributed to subscribers in one hundred nations around the world.

After becoming an Airline Transport Rated pilot, I built a substantial multifaceted aviation business. After helplessly watching that business fail, I built a second large, multifaceted organization that is presently quite successful.

Although I have not learned all there is to know about success, or the traps that can bring failure, through these experiences I have learned a great deal that could be helpful to anyone on a significant life journey. In addition to achieving most of my own personal goals to date, I have been blessed throughout my life to meet some of the most successful people in business, sports, politics, the military, arts and religion. Some I have been privileged to know quite well. It has been one of my life's goals to understand great accomplishments and the people who achieve them. My observations of successful people have led to some very unique and interesting conclusions about leadership, creativity, and management that are simple and workable in any situation from a family to an international corporation.

In all that I have experienced and observed, it has become obvious to me that the patterns required for success are always the same, and they are simple. Failure is much more complicated. If you have the intelligence to read and understand this simple book, you can succeed in life, you can be a leader, and you can do it with creativity that will impact many others.

If you have picked up this book and have read this far, it is likely that you have at least a hope of doing something significant with your life, or you have already been successful and something is driving you to reach for greater heights. Regardless, this book can help you. Before going on, settle in your heart that despite your present conditions, you can succeed, and as long as you live you can continue to go higher and higher. You have probably heard the fearful and earthbound say that if man were meant to fly he would have been given wings. Man *has* been given wings, but they are in our minds and hearts. This book is to help you learn to use them, soaring above the ordinary and usual to live on the heights of the earth.

—The Author

CHAPTER ONE

THE FOUNDATION OF POWER

Power is the ability to exert force to accomplish a purpose. Of all the ways this can be done, leadership is the most powerful. Those who understand the basic principles of leadership are the ones who shape the world we live in, and in a very real sense, rule over it. Those who do not understand leadership and do not use it will be subject to those who do.

This book is a study of the basic principles of leadership that rule the world. The principles of leadership are easy to understand, but they are not as easy to implement. If you learn them, and have the resolve to use them, you will almost certainly accomplish your purpose. If you do not, it is unlikely that you will accomplish anything of significance.

Because using the principles of leadership requires inspiration and courage, I have added to this study some of the most lucid and interesting examples of how they were used successfully in history. Many of these examples are from epic military battles. Almost every successful life can be defined as a series of battles fought, with an ultimate victory achieved. Military battles also have such extreme consequences, with the potential to be life or death for everyone involved, so they tend to highlight the best and worst examples of leadership. However, these same principles can be found in the building of a business, sports team, mission, or a church.

WHAT IS A LEADER?

No one is a leader unless someone is following. Therefore, leadership is the ability to mobilize others to accomplish a common goal. Successful leadership is vision combined with the resolve, courage, and endurance that it takes to accomplish the goal, to press the job until it is finished.

There will always be leadership. Whenever there is an absence of leadership, it will quickly be filled by someone. If the noble do not rule, the profane will. The best men and women in history, as well as the most evil, have used the same principles of leadership. If evil prevails in a place or time, it is because the initiative is seized while the good wavered. When good prevails, it is because the good seize the initiative and lead.

It has been said that there are three kinds of people in the world:

1. Those who make things happen.
2. Those who watch things happen.
3. Those who wonder what's happening.

Leaders are made from those who know what is happening, and are not content to sit on the sidelines of life and watch others determine their affairs. They recognize opportunities and seize them with boldness. Leaders are the ones who *make* things happen.

A study made by Richard Leider and David Shapiro found that the number one fear people have is to live a meaningless life. Defining one's purpose and fulfilling it is the deepest yearning of the human soul. We were created in the image of God, and just as He set out to do great and marvelous things, so is there a spark in every human soul to do the same. The spark is there, but what will we do with it? The principles addressed in this book will separate those who accomplish their purpose from those who pass through their lives just dreaming about it, or worse, complaining about it.

The yearning to do something of significance is greater than just attaining fame or fortune. Those who seek fame and fortune seldom attain such. These are shallow goals that keep those who are preoccupied by them from doing anything of significance. However, those who have a vision, and the resolve to fulfill it, usually gain both fame and fortune.

A leader must move with purpose. The more clear and specific the purpose, the more boldly a leader can move forward. The world will be drawn to those who know where they are going. People will only follow as long as you proceed with conviction and resolve to fulfill your purpose. Therefore, keeping your purposes ever before you is fundamental if you are to continue to mobilize and motivate. As Laurie Beth Jones stated in her book, *The Path,* "People with a clearly defined mission have always led those who do not have one. You are either living your mission, or you are living someone else's."

THE PASSION OF PURPOSE

Most people are like worker bees who devote themselves to helping fulfill someone else's vision. However, worker bees that labor with resolve and conviction can also be elevated to the greatness of fulfillment. A primary step required for the development of true leadership is to understand that there are no insignificant tasks. The people who become the greatest at great things began by being great at little things. Those who do great things have greatness in them, and they do everything by a higher standard, even the seemingly insignificant tasks. If you will do whatever you are doing now with all your heart, and face every task with that passion and devotion to excellence, you will do great things because greatness will be in you. You may feel and be unappreciated for a time, but if you continue to do everything with excellence, in due time your greatness will be known.

Underachievers usually spend their lives dreaming about the day their "big break" will come, believing their true greatness will then become known to the world. For them life is like a lottery. One in ten million will get such a break, enjoy their short-lived fame, and then burn out like a cheap firecracker.

True achievers do not play such a lottery, or waste their time dreaming about it. They build their lives with strategy and vision. If you do not have a purpose that is the focus and drive of your life, it is the aim of this book to first help you find it, and then devise a clear and workable plan for fulfilling it.

AN ENEMY CALLED "EASY"

The basic principles that make one an achiever in any field are the same. The reason so few fulfill their potential is because there are obstacles on the paths that lead to all significant achievements. These obstacles can keep the most gifted people from achieving even clearly defined purposes, unless they have the resolve, courage, and endurance to overcome the trials and problems that stand in their way.

These obstacles seem intentionally placed in this world to make accomplishments difficult. However, what makes something valuable is that it is either hard to find or hard to get. Few things that are worthwhile have ever been easily achieved. Those who run from difficulties lack the fortitude one must have to be a leader in this world. If you are looking for an easy formula for success, you are studying the wrong subject. The path to success is never without difficulties but true leaders will overcome them.

If you are going to fulfill your purpose you must first determine to be a fighter, and that quitting is not an option. We will examine common obstacles that everyone with vision seems to face. Understanding them can help if you care enough for your purpose to fight for it. If the fight is not in you, either your purpose is not worthy or you are not worthy of your purpose. If you determine that your purpose is worth fighting for, then learn how to fight because obstacles will come. It will not be easy but it will be worth it.

In a world that is increasingly addicted to convenience and ease, it may take more resolve to become an achiever of great things today than it did in years past. However, it seems that the rewards are also greater than ever for those who have such resolve. Understanding the obstacles that every achiever faces is half the battle to overcoming them. Even so, after a few victories, battles will no longer be faced with dread. After tasting the rewards of victory that come from the fight, you will begin to love the battle that alone can lead to victory. Fighting will then actually become half the fun. The struggle is meant to make you great so that you can do great things. Every battle is an opportunity for victory and an opportunity for growth in character that will prepare you for greater battles and greater victories.

This study is not about information, but transformation. Even if we have already been successful, we must continue to ask how we can be even more successful. Anything that has stopped growing has started dying. Our goal in life must be to excel more and more. If we have suffered failures, one of our greatest achievements of all is to not let them stop us, but rather increase our resolve until ultimate victory is achieved.

Those who have suffered some of the greatest failures, and did not quit, became some of the greatest leaders of all. It does not matter where you fit into this picture now; your goal must be to go higher. That is why this is a study of the characteristics that are needed to be successful, as well as the stumbling blocks that will attempt to thwart our success.

Stumbling blocks, when understood, can become our greatest stepping-stones to success. Thomas Edison failed at one thousand experiments before he succeeded in developing the light bulb. He was not discouraged by the failures, but recorded them, and learned from them. He knew that every one of them was necessary for his ultimate achievement. We too must learn to make the most of our failures and defeats. The wisdom gained from them will probably be required for our ultimate success.

MY CREDENTIALS

What are my credentials for writing such a book? I have proven in my own life what is written here. I have a history of significant achievements and successes. To date every goal that I have set in my life has been accomplished. There are still bigger ones before me, but I do have a track record of success.

I have also had significant and devastating failures. I have achieved wealth, and suffered bankruptcy. I have navigated through hundreds of seemingly life-and-death decisions to build a unique business, just to have one bad choice undo it all. I will be as candid about such failures as I am about the successes. There is a minefield to cross on the way to any worthy success, and now I know where many of the mines are located. The truly wise will learn as much as they can from both the successes and failures of others, realizing that they will have enough obstacles to overcome without adding those they could avoid. If you are wise you will not try to cover up your own mistakes, but view them as opportunities to add to your resources the most valuable treasure of all—wisdom.

I have had my dreams shot to pieces a number of times. I have stood on the pinnacle of success only to find that the pinnacle itself was a mine that was ready to explode when I stepped on it. Even so, I got back on my feet to find another path up the mountain. Every failure has ultimately led me to the path of an even greater success. I do not consider these successes the result of being smarter or better than others, but mainly the result of the conviction that God's grace comes to those who humble themselves enough to acknowledge and learn from their mistakes, while maintaining the resolve not to quit.

If you are humble enough to be teachable, courageous enough to face your battles head on, and have the endurance to keep going regardless of how hard it gets, you will ultimately stand in the place of victory.

CHAPTER TWO

THE POWER OF MOVEMENT

In the biblical account, God's instrument of creation, the Holy Spirit, was moving. Movement is required for creativity and accomplishment. This is probably why the great trends that have set the course of history are often called "movements." Nothing happens for those who sit and dream. If we are to accomplish our purposes, we must learn how to start moving and then keep moving.

Water that is not moving becomes stagnant very fast. The same is true of human life. To keep moving requires willingness to continually leave comfort and security behind. We must not become addicted to our comfort zones but learn to be secure and bold in the place of risk. The insecure will never accomplish great things. John Wimber, a great evangelist of the 1980s used to say, "Faith is spelled R-I-S-K." John lived this belief and raised up hundreds of churches all over the world, starting a movement that spanned the globe. He did this at a time when such ministries were not held in very high esteem.

If you have experienced defeat in such a way that you are afraid to try again, this book can help you start going again. Staying where you are is not an option. To stay where you are is a worse prison than suffering another defeat. Those who do not suffer defeats are those who are not in the fight. If you are not in the fight of life, you are no longer alive but just exist.

If you try to go forward you may get hurt again, but that is not the worst thing that can happen to you. The worst thing of all is to pass out of this life knowing that you did not accomplish what you could have. As the proverb states, "A coward dies a thousand deaths, but the courageous will die only once." Take courage. Regardless of your present situation, there is a way out. However, the door can be found only by those who live by faith—"R-I-S-K."

Fear is our most deadly enemy. It will fight us the whole way. Courage is not the absence of fear, but it is the resolve to not let fear dictate what we do. If we let fear dictate our course we will not reach our goal. The path to success is marked for those who see with the eyes of courage. Success does not keep cowards for companions, and this book is not written for the timid. I am not writing to make you feel good, but to tell you the truth that will enable you to fulfill your purpose.

I have been privileged to meet some of the most successful people in a diversity fields. I have observed success from many vantage points. I have come to understand that the reasons for success are the same in every case, and they are strikingly simple.

Leo Tolstoy, possibly the greatest novelist who ever lived, began one of his classic novels, *Anna Karenina*, with a profound insight: "Every happy family is alike. Every unhappy family is unhappy in its own way." We might also say that the secret to success is always the same, but failure is much more complicated. The principles for success are basic and simple. If you try to make them more complicated than they are, you will begin to fall into traps which are often fittingly called "complications."

THE TRUE NOBILITY

Along with the very successful people that I have been privileged to know, I have also met a number of people from the noble families of Europe. Some of these have been stripped of their titles, possessions, and even their history by communism. Even so, they could not be stripped of their noble character. Communism died, but nobility didn't. Like the famous television saga, *Roots*, these individuals kept their purpose alive by keeping their history alive and now they have a future again.

Nobility itself has been an abused institution in history. Many noble families were anything but noble in character. True nobility is not just having titles, property, or influence. Rather it is the vision for nobility that is crucial to establishing families that will remain noble generation after generation. Alex Haley's *Roots* articulates the tremendous truth that true nobility can be found in a family of slaves compelled by a noble purpose. For that family, it was freedom that kept them on a course of destiny for generation after generation until it was achieved. Having a noble purpose will bring out the best in us, and can be passed on to our children.

The issue of freedom will be found intertwined with every truly noble purpose. As one of the great apostles wrote, "where the Spirit of the Lord is there is liberty." In the very beginning God established this principle when He planted the Tree of the Knowledge of Good and Evil in the Garden of Eden. God told the man not to eat from it, but then gave him the freedom to choose. He did not do this to cause the fall of man, but because there can be no true obedience unless there is freedom to disobey. In the same way, there can be no true worship unless there is freedom not to worship. We cannot be who we were created to be without freedom, and like the family in *Roots*, who never gave up, this must be a basic quest in our lives. It is always right to fight for freedom.

We are free to do right or wrong, but we must also understand that our choice has consequences. Men like to blame the evil in the world on God, but all evil is the result of choices men make. From the beginning God gave man the authority to rule over the earth and nowhere do we see that He has taken it back. Consequences are required if there is to be responsibility, and without responsibility there can be no true authority. Therefore, responsibility is also one of the most basic characteristics of leadership. If our goal is truly noble then we must be committed to using noble means to accomplish it. What good is it to accomplish the greatest goals if we lose the nobility of our character in the process?

Freedom is a basic characteristic required for the true development of the human soul. The freedom that we must have to be who we were created to be cannot be given or taken away by a government. Governments can make it easier or harder for people to accomplish their goals, but they cannot dictate who we are in our hearts. We can be a slave and be free if our vision is greater than our chains. We can be free, wealthy, and powerful, and still be a slave if our fears are greater than our vision. True nobility of character is not dependent upon our environment, but upon what is within us.

As Charles Dickens wrote, "These are the best of times, and the worst of times." There seems to be an unprecedented assault upon every moral principle of character and nobility in these times. This seemingly unprecedented assault on values can be the finest hour for the truly noble. Those with destiny and purpose can rise higher than ever because their light shines brighter in darkness.

LIGHT HAS POWER

Those who have the light within will know the course through any approaching darkness, and find the way to a bright new day. When you open your shades at night, darkness does not come into the room, but rather light shines out into the darkness. Light is more powerful than darkness, and light will ultimately prevail. Now is the time to find that light, and your light through the future will be found in your purpose.

For you to have picked up a book like this is an indication that you are not meant to be one of the "worker bees," who are the majority of people who go through life unfulfilled, frustrated, and bored. It does not matter how old you are, or how complicated your life is now; your life can become a success story. You can also leave a heritage of accomplishment that is passed on to future generations. You can do more than just read about other people's success stories—your life can become one of them.

If you become one of the truly noble, you can pass the resolve and character that is in you on to your children, who will likewise pass it on to their children. You will also infect the nobility of purpose in others who come to know you. True nobility is infectious, and it will spread to those who come in contact with it. We are living in a time when there is a meltdown of morality and integrity, which makes it an even greater time for the truly noble to arise.

You were made in the image of God, so there is a very high calling on your life. Just as His Spirit had to be moving in order to create, we too need to be moving for the power of creativity to be released through our lives. Creativity is a basic characteristic of leadership. We are not leaders unless we are going somewhere. We must keep moving.

CHAPTER THREE

THE ACHIEVERS

I was once sitting in Reggie White's den listening to him and a team mate from the Green Bay Packers discuss their football careers. Reggie is almost universally acknowledged to be one of the best to ever play the game. He is also a member of the Hall of Fame. Listening to Reggie and his teammate talk, I was surprised to hear their light bantering become more serious. One of them remarked that many of the young men they had known could have been outstanding players. They also said that there were probably kids in every city who could have been better than they were, but never even suited up for an organized game of football though they dreamed about it daily. Is this true? Why do so many who have the potential to become great at their heart's desire, fail to be successful? Why do so many even fail to enter the game?

It is true that those who could be the greatest in every field never fulfill their potential. Most who have the talent to be great musicians will spend their lives listening to others perform. The greatest potential businessmen, artists, scientists, statesmen, doctors, lawyers, writers, and ministers will probably spend their lives doing something that they are bored with, and never do what they were given the talent to do. Why? Because they failed to understand the simple principles that make the difference between living a fruitful, fulfilling life, or a life of failure and frustration.

The following are five characteristics that are found in the lives of most successful people:

1. They define their goal.

2. They stay focused on their goal.

3. They have the wisdom and resolve to gather the necessary resources, or training, to accomplish their goal.

4. They do not associate with "problem oriented people," but surround themselves with "solution oriented people."

5. They refuse to let obstacles stop them or change their course.

This book is intended to help you apply these basic principles to your particular situation. We will look at a number of examples that illustrate each principle from different perspectives. Each example contains new insights while maintaining a simplicity that can help you apply them to your own situation.

Knowing these principles can help, but that alone is not enough. They must go beyond mere principles and become our nature. This requires repetition, which is often boring, but necessary if we are going to succeed. To be truly successful we must rise above the common malady of having to be constantly entertained with something new and different, and learn to be constant. It is for this reason that some of the basic principles in this book are repeated. This is not a mistake—my goal is not to entertain you, or to make you think this is a good book. It is to help you achieve your purpose.

IT IS YOUR DESTINY

To have a destiny implies that there is a Supreme Being who created you for a purpose. Any intelligent person knows that modern science has established beyond any reasonable doubt that God certainly exists. That may be a surprising statement to you, but true science and true faith have always been in agreement. Pseudo science starts with the conclusion that God does not exist and bends all its findings to prove this premise. There is room to debate who has the most accurate theology to explain what God is like, and what He expects of us, but the fact that He exists is obvious to any rational person. As a professor once said, "The harmony of nature is so complex, so interrelated, that the odds are better that a tornado could hit a junk yard and leave behind a perfectly built 747 jumbo jet than for the earth as it is to have just happened by chance."

One scientist explained that if the earth were either closer or further from the sun by the equivalent of just one eighth of an inch over a one hundred mile distance we would either freeze or fry! The odds that the earth's orbit just happened to accidentally get caught in that tiny little slice of space where life could be supported is beyond any logical person's consideration. Then we must add the fact that if the earth did not tilt on its axis exactly as it does, ice would form all on one side and the earth would wobble out of this little slice of orbit where our lives can be sustained.

The odds that any one of these things could have happened by random chance is beyond reason. But when you start stacking all these unfathomably intricate and interrelated foundations of life as we know it on top of each other, it would take a book many times larger than this just to list them all. Anyone of true intellectual honesty understands that *we are not alone!* There is a God with intelligence far beyond the power of all of our computers linked together. He made the universe with beauty, grace, and purpose. He obviously loves detail and diversity.

The Creator is obviously creative. In the Bible account of creation, men were made in the image of God. That is why there is a basic drive within you to be creative, and to do something significant with your creativity. You were made this way and you will not be fulfilled until you have used the talent you have been given. Jesus said that, "Out of your innermost being will flow rivers of living water," or that which is truly alive must come from your heart. Basically, what you really want to do in your heart of hearts or your "innermost being," is the very thing you were created to do.

The first step toward fulfilling your purpose is to be yourself. The whole world will try to fashion you into what it wants you to be, but true leaders resist this bondage and determine to make their world what they want it to be. You were created for a purpose, and you will find it by discovering the deepest desire of your heart.

If being an athlete is the passion of your heart, you must now determine that you are going to spend more time practicing and working out than watching others play. If it is in your heart to be a musician, you must determine now to spend more time practicing your instrument than listening to others. You must determine right now that you are not going to waste time dreaming about doing. You must have a dream, but once you have it you must not spend any more time dreaming. You are called to be a doer!

One major difference between achievers and dreamers is that achievers turn the drudgery of practice into a passionate opportunity to grow in excellence. It does not matter how good your natural talents are, if you practice them you will be much better. To be as good as you can be, every practice must be treated as if you are playing before the King. If you truly love what you are doing, you will love practicing it too.

My associate, Steve Thompson, once said, "Anything worth doing is worth doing poorly." This has nothing to do with being devoted to excellence, but instead the reality of what it takes to begin any endeavor. The best pianist to ever play started playing poorly. The best quarterback to ever play a game was not very good when he first threw a football. Both were probably embarrassed if anyone was watching them, but they pressed on. They endured the mistakes, the bad notes, and the seemingly endless repetition, until one day they started doing it better. Then they persevered to excel even more. No one rises to the top without taking the first step, and then continuing to put one foot in front of the other for as long as it takes. They try to be as great when no one is looking as they are when playing before vast crowds, because greatness is their nature.

CHAPTER FOUR

DEVELOPING THE FIVE ESSENTIALS FOR SUCCESS

In this chapter the five common characteristics of successful people will be addressed in a little more detail. If we are going to succeed, these must become as basic to our nature as the devotion to excellence.

FACTOR NUMBER ONE: YOU MUST DEFINE YOUR GOAL.

If you could do one thing and be guaranteed that you would not fail, what would it be? Believe it or not, the answer to this question is probably what you were given the talent to do with your life. You may need to adjust some of your reasons for wanting to do it, and how you would do it, but your answer to this question can be an important clue to help you define your overall goal in life.

Before we can do what we have the talent(s) to do, we need to get specific. *Those who have goals that are too general rarely accomplish them.* Those who want to "go into business for themselves" almost never do. Those who want to "be a musician" or "go into politics" almost never do, or if they do they quickly fail. However, those who go into business because they love a certain product or service are much more likely to succeed. Those who fall in love with a specific musical instrument are much more likely to become successful musicians.

Those who go into politics because of a specific cause are more likely to succeed in politics.

STEP NUMBER ONE FOR SUCCESS IS TO *CLEARLY* DEFINE YOUR GOAL.

FACTOR NUMBER TWO:
YOU MUST STAY FOCUSED ON YOUR GOAL.

I was once asked to speak to the Denver Broncos before an important Monday night football game. The focus, resolution, and determination on the faces of those players were greater than I had ever seen on any audience. I knew that this was the look of success—*focus.* I was later asked to speak to the New Orleans Saints before a game. That team also had players with remarkable focus on their faces—but it was only evident on about a third of the players. I felt that they were in danger of losing that day, and they did. The level of our success will be determined by the level of our focus. Likewise, as leaders, the level of our success will be determined by the level of focus that we can instill in those who are following us.

I once visited the home of a friend who played for the Washington Redskins, to attend a game they were playing against their chief rival, the Dallas Cowboys. Even though it was a home game, my friend had to spend the night before the game in a hotel with the team so they could stay focused. After years of training just to get to the professional level, they still spent hours each day practicing, studying plays, and studying their opponents. As game day approached they separated themselves from potential outside distractions. Once you reach the pinnacle of success, you will remain there only as long as you are willing to stay focused, and keep working.

Focus itself is a great skill. Once we are focused, we must have the discipline to stay focused. This probably does not come naturally to anyone—it is a discipline to which we must train ourselves. Without this discipline, we are not likely to make it to the ranks of the achievers.

The diversions that distract us from the purposes of our lives can come from positive or negative factors. Many cannot see past the obstacles to attain their goal, so they are tempted to seek easier goals. As Harry Truman observed, "Many people are defeated by secondary success." There are probably as many people diverted from their ultimate goals by a success in a lesser purpose, as there are those who give up because of difficulties.

Albert Einstein stated, "Premature responsibility breeds superficiality." Martin Lloyd-Jones, one of the great theologians of the twentieth century said that premature success is one of the most dangerous things that can happen to a person. Any goal that is accomplished too quickly or too easily is probably not a significant accomplishment. Determine that you are in this for the long haul. The accomplishment of any worthy goal will be more of a marathon than a sprint.

After you have determined your goal you must determine that you will not be diverted from it until it is achieved. Recite that goal in your heart every day. Write it on something that you can look at daily. Your ultimate purpose is worthy of your attention every day. If you are not drawn to it daily in some way, it has probably not yet been set in your heart the way it must be if you are going to accomplish it.

FACTOR NUMBER THREE:
YOU MUST GATHER THE NECESSARY RESOURCES, OR TRAINING, FOR ACCOMPLISHING YOUR GOAL.

When you have a clear vision of your purpose, and the resolve to stay focused on it, you are much more likely to see all that will be required for fulfilling it. The fulfillment of every goal requires preparation, usually in the form of training, education, and practice.

To gather the necessary resources for accomplishing your goal means that you must have a plan. The more significant the goal, the more preparation and planning are usually required. The better the plan, the more likely you are to accomplish the goal. The ability to plan is a rare skill, but few ever accomplish anything without it.

One of my earliest goals in life was to become a professional aircraft pilot. One of the first things I was taught in flight training was how important it is to develop a good flight plan. As I graduated to bigger and faster aircrafts, the more important the planning became. When I moved to jets, the flight plans had to be much more carefully laid out and studied because we were covering ground too fast to do much recalculating in the air. If changes were needed, I would have already thought them through on the ground so they were almost automatic. The better my planning skills became, the better pilot I was.

Accomplishing any worthwhile goal is going to be difficult, but we do not want it to be unnecessarily hard. We should try to make it as easy as possible so that unplanned difficulties can be handled without over-taxing our abilities. Developing good planning skills is crucial for this reason. As the old proverb states, "Those who fail to plan, plan to fail."

The main difference between star athletes, musicians, artists, or great professionals in any field, and those who have similar talents but are sitting in the audience, is simply the ability to focus on their goal, and the devotion to train, practice, and prepare. We are thrilled by the ballplayer who wins the World Series with a single swing of his bat. But just to get in that position he had to spend thousands of hours swinging his bat in practice, enduring the heat, boredom, and blisters day after day, week after week, and year after year. For every second that Olympic athletes spend performing their event, they have probably spent thousands of hours in training. If you want to go to the highest level, that is the price you will have to pay. As Lee Trevino said after someone remarked that he had made a lucky shot, "Yeah, it may have been lucky, but the more I practice the luckier I get!"

There is no doubt that the average person's life would be much more fruitful and fulfilling, not to mention easier, if they took the time to develop good planning skills. For everything worthwhile that we do, we need a plan. The more important or difficult the goal, the more planning we must do. Like a good flight plan, we need checkpoints along the way. These checkpoints are mini-goals that we need to accomplish along the way to our ultimate goal. It is always fulfilling to reach these checkpoints, but they are not our final destinations, so we must not take too much time celebrating them.

As a pilot, one of the most important items in the flight plan is to determine how much fuel is needed to arrive at our destination, along with the reserves that might be needed for emergencies, un-forecasted bad weather, or other contingencies. The possibility of unforeseen events is a basic reason we make a plan for our goal as well. We must gather the necessary resources to accomplish our goal while allowing for potential diversions.

As a pilot, another important factor that determines how much fuel I need are the weather conditions. I have to consider the present conditions that are being reported, along with how they could change during the time of my flight. Will there be thunderstorms that I will need to circumnavigate? Will I have to shoot an instrument approach at my destination? Could the conditions potentially be so bad at my destination that I will have to deviate to an alternate airport, and if so, which is the closest one that is likely to have suitable conditions to land? Will the air traffic be so heavy at my destination that I might have to be put in a holding pattern for a period of time? All of these factors could determine the amount of fuel needed. It is necessary to check the conditions being reported at my destination, as well as conditions of vicinities close to my destination. The more thorough my preparation, the more confidently I can make necessary adjustments to the plan when they are required.

FACTOR NUMBER FOUR: SURROUND YOURSELF WITH SOLUTION ORIENTED PEOPLE.

One of the first steps that successful leaders will almost always take when assuming a new position is to get rid of everyone who spends more time talking about problems than about solutions.

When General Grant took over the Union Army of the Potomac during the Civil War, it had already suffered many defeats at the hands of General Lee and his Confederate Army. The officers and men had become conditioned by these defeats. When Grant first marched against Lee even his commanders warned him repeatedly of impending doom. In his first engagement with Lee, at the Battle of the Wilderness, reports came in from every division that they were beaten. All day long Grant's officers begged him to flee to the safety of Washington before Lee cut them off from their path of retreat. Finally, when it was obvious even to Grant that they had been soundly beaten, as his officers waited for the orders to retreat, Grant astonished them all by giving orders to turn South and advance on to Richmond!

When his generals begged him to reconsider, assuring him they were doomed if they did not flee immediately, Grant dismissed them and retreated to the solitude of his own tent. He confided to a reporter that he had never been in a battle where at some point it did not look like they would be defeated, but he believed that in every crisis there was some opportunity for victory. This belief enabled him to see that if Lee tried to cut off his retreat to Washington, it would actually enable him to do something that every other Union general had tried to do and failed—to get his army between Lee and Richmond so that he could advance on the Southern capitol. His "defeat" at the Battle of the Wilderness actually opened the door for his greatest opportunity.

When Lee heard that Grant was not retreating after such a sound defeat, but was marching South, he confided to his generals that the end of the Confederacy was near. When the Union troops started marching South, a great cheer went up from their ranks. For the first time they had a general who would fight. Lee would paste several more defeats on Grant, but never once did Grant consider retreating. Never once did he pay attention to the doomsayers. He probably never did win an outright battle against Lee, but he held his course until he won the war.

At the Battle of the Wilderness, Grant dismissed the doomsayers on his staff so that those who were left got a loud and clear message— they were there to look for ways to win, not ways to avoid defeat. The ones who were left were optimistic, solution-oriented leaders who understood that faith equaled risk. One of the basic principles for every successful leader to understand is that to win and accomplish your goals, you must get rid of the people on your team who are more focused on the problems than the solutions.

In the biblical account of the Israelites journey to the Promised Land, they sent spies to check it out before beginning their conquest. Two of the spies came back and said, "No problem, we can take it." Ten of the spies returned with frightening stories about how big the people were, and how well their cities were fortified. This report was true, but they added that it would be impossible for them to conquer the land. The people listened to the ten who were fearful, and spent forty years wandering in circles in the wilderness until that whole generation perished. Most people today likewise spend their lives going in circles, never fulfilling their potential, and never reaching their promised land because they listen more to the fearful than to those who are faithful. Faithful means "full of faith." If you are going to fulfill your destiny, it will take courage. Surround yourself with courageous people.

FACTOR NUMBER FIVE:
REFUSE TO LET OBSTACLES STOP YOU OR DIVERT YOU FROM YOUR COURSE.

Some of the factors that can help you attain your goals in life can be controlled, and some cannot. Factors that can be controlled include such disciplines as hard work, defined goals, staying focused on your goals, and attaining the necessary resources to achieve them.

Perhaps the greatest single factor in releasing the highest levels of human achievement is one that we cannot control, and will usually do everything that we can to avoid—*adversity*.

Great success usually comes at a great price. What comes cheaply usually has little value. Successful people in every field are those who refuse to be stopped. You are not going to get where you are going without problems—no one does. The world is not fair so do not be surprised when you are not treated fairly. Every bad thing that happens to you can either make you bitter or make you better. Bitter people never win. Determine that you will get better and that every mountain you must climb is there to make you stronger. Those who stay resolutely on the course to fulfilling their goals regardless of setbacks and disappointments are the greatest achievers.

The eagle is considered one of the noblest birds. Few can soar to the heights that eagles reach. It has been said that all of nature fears storms except the eagle. That is because eagles know if they approach opposing winds at the proper angle they can be carried to even greater heights with less effort. Remember, every opposing wind is an opportunity to go higher, but you must approach it at the right angle, or with the right attitude.

One primary delusion about accomplishment is the belief that some become achievers because they had favorable circumstances, and they got the "big break." Using that as an excuse is one of the main reasons why many fail. The obstacles that confronted Reggie White, and almost every other player in any professional sport were usually as great as those facing everyone else. Very few achievers in any field are given special breaks. In fact, when special breaks are given to those with great ability, it often works to their detriment, causing them to fall short of fulfilling their true potential.

When Reggie went out for high school football, he was the only player that was constantly picked on by his coach. At times he was even punched and physically abused. One day he finally asked the coach why he was so mean to him and not the others. The coach replied that he had asked the parents of every player for permission to do this, and his mother was the only one who agreed. Reggie was mad at his mother for a while, but now he knows that he would have never been the player that he became without her wisdom in allowing the coach to make it harder for him. She knew that the temporary pain and embarrassment would make him much better, and it did.

We may dread difficulties when they come, but they will make us better. The Russian writer, Aleksander V. Solzhenitsyn, once made the observation that "Even biology teaches us that perpetual well-being is not good for any creature." Adversity does more for our development than possibly any other single factor. Adversity helps us to focus, eliminate the non-essentials, and devote ourselves to what is really important. Adversity will cause the truly devoted to work even harder, thus becoming stronger and better. If success comes too easily, we will grow weaker because of it.

Knowing this is true, and that our purpose is to reach our goal, it is not wrong to want to get there as free of obstacles as possible. We want to avoid unnecessary problems, but we must also have the resolve to overcome any that do come, and seize them as opportunities for growth.

I greatly appreciate modern conveniences, but I also recognize that it is easy to become dangerously addicted to convenience. I have golfed with many friends who try one new club or ball after another seeking the "magic remedy" that will improve their game. As Lee Trevino said in a commercial for a new golf ball, "This ball really can help you improve your game, if you will hit three hundred of them a day!"

Now, before going any further, get a sheet of paper and write down how the following five characteristics apply to you.

1. What is your goal?

2. What do you need to do to focus on this goal?

3. What resources or training will you need to accomplish your goal?

4. Are there negative people around you who spend more time talking about what is wrong than about possibilities? How are you going to replace these friends or associates with positive ones?

5. What obstacles do you foresee that could prevent you from achieving your goal? How are you going to overcome them?

Keep this piece of paper. Read it every day, taking time to ponder each part. Take care of it because one day you will want to frame it.

CHAPTER FIVE

HABITUAL SUCCESS

Ricky Skaggs is one of my best friends. When I met him he was at the pinnacle of success as a country music singer. He then ran into seemingly insurmountable obstacles that caused him to slide from his position at the top. Never getting bitter, he used each setback as an opportunity to evaluate his future goals, and to chart a course to even greater success, which he has now accomplished.

Ricky was a child prodigy. He was only six years old when Bill Monroe, the man considered the father of bluegrass music, lifted him up on stage to play with him. Bill Monroe was a perfectionist as a musician, and anyone who shared the stage with him had to be one of the best. At the age of only six years, Ricky was already good enough to play with the best.

As everyone expected, Ricky went on to become known as one of the best guitar pickers to ever come to Nashville. He was also one of the best mandolin and fiddle players. His music was loved by just about everyone including those who did not usually like country music. His number one hits and top ten hits mounted up. Then while accepting The CMA Entertainer of the Year Award in 1985, he went beyond the politically correct to acknowledge God, and thanked Jesus for giving him the gift to make music. People were offended. Even though his next releases were considered to be his best yet, they did not make it into the stores in sufficient numbers to become hits, or receive the radio play that almost everyone thought they deserved.

Ricky accepted these setbacks as providential, and started looking for a way to turn this defeat into an even greater victory. He found more than one. He started one of the most popular country music television shows called, "At the Ryman with Ricky Skaggs." At the time, country music was the hottest music on the planet.

Then Ricky took one of the biggest risks of his life. Musicians commonly use gospel and bluegrass music as stepping-stones to try to break into country music. Ricky loved country music, but he loved bluegrass and gospel even more. He determined that he was going to sing and play the music that he loved the most, not just what was popular at the time. Going the opposite direction of everyone else seeking success in Nashville, he started his own gospel and bluegrass labels so he could sing what he wanted and produced other artists that he chose. The music world watched, and most were shocked by his success.

To date, every project on his bluegrass label "Skaggs Family Records" has been a hit. He has received three more Grammys, and is doing better financially than he ever did recording for others. Top artists are lining up to sign with him because his contracts are fair. When I had breakfast with Ricky recently, he was pondering an offer from one of the world's top movie and music producing companies. They were offering him big bucks for just a fraction of his new labels. This is the dream of most label owners, but Ricky was about to turn them down because he just did not have peace about it.

It is also interesting to note that country music has been sliding in popularity while both gospel and bluegrass music are rising. By following his heart, Ricky did not just catch a new wave—he helped create one. Now, although Ricky has reached the age when most fall into increasing obscurity, it is obvious that his best days are still ahead of him. Even more important to him than staying on the pinnacle is his desire to do what is in his heart, and he just keeps getting better.

No one stays at the pinnacle of success forever, and most do not stay there very long. However, when your slide begins, it is seldom wise to strive to stay at the top. Remember the lessons you learned that enabled you to get there, and then look for another path to use them again. Many people take risks when they have nothing to lose, but those who take them when they are already successful are the only ones who have a realistic chance of continued success. Above all, follow your heart.

CHAPTER SIX

THE END OF TRENCH WARFARE

True leadership is always of a new breed because following old paths is not leading, it is following. General John J. Pershing, who commanded the U.S. Forces in World War I, is one of the great and remarkable examples of a new breed of leadership. When the Spanish American War broke out, Pershing was thirty-eight years old and still a 1st Lieutenant. Many of the great generals in history were younger than he was. Even so, he did not complain about being overlooked, but determined to be the best 1st Lieutenant in the army.

Pershing was awarded a Silver Star for gallantry because of the charge he led up San Juan Hill, and was promoted to captain. He remained a captain until he was forty-four. While serving in the Philippines, when the other officers spent their time enjoying the sunset from their verandas, Pershing studied. He studied the nation he was serving, their history, culture, and language—anything that might help him to be a better soldier in his assignment. This is a prominent factor in the life of every great leader: During the lulls in action, or long years of waiting until their time, *THEY DO NOT WASTE THEIR TIME.*

The time that Pershing spent waiting did not sap his resolve but galvanized it. Even if he had remained a captain, he was determined to be the best captain in the army, prepared for whatever his country might need him for. This incredible patience of Pershing finally paid off. When Teddy Roosevelt became President, he remembered Pershing from San Juan Hill, and promoted him past a host of other officers all the way to Brigadier General. Just a little over a year later, the United States entered World War I, and Pershing was promoted again, becoming the Supreme Commander of the United States Expeditionary Forces in Europe. The man who had just recently been a junior officer leading a single company was about to lead two million men into one of the most important battles in history.

It was said of Pershing that even when he was a lieutenant he carried himself like a general. Although he always saw himself as a general, during the many long years that could have been the supreme frustration of a man of his ability, he did not complain or waste away in bitterness—he just kept preparing for the day that he would be needed. Because of this when his time came, he was ready and would have to be included on the short list of the greatest military leaders in history.

When the Americans entered World War I, the British and French Allies had been bogged down in a demoralizing and costly trench warfare for nearly three years. Millions had died in meaningless attacks to take a few hundred yards of ground, which would inevitably be given back again in a counter-attack. Is this not the state of many industries, governments, and churches? Many are stalemated and confined to what amounts to trench warfare. It is big news when any ground is taken but then it is quickly lost again.

When you're in the trenches, if you stick your head up a little higher than anyone else to try to see, you will be shot at. If anyone today tries to rise above the confines in which everyone else is wasting away, they will quickly become the target of a multitude of jealous accusers and slanderers. We too have an enemy who is doing all that he can to keep us pinned down in the trenches. It is a victory for him to keep us stalemated. It is often a victory for us just to raise our heads enough to see a little farther than others.

The British and French armies were near exhaustion when America entered the war. The entire strategy of the Allied leadership was to try to find replacements for their casualties, which were many. No one could see a way out. The only hope of the Allies was to outlast the Germans and have a few men left when Germany finally ran out. After the revolution, when Russia made peace with Germany, suddenly it was the Germans who had fresh reinforcements from their now quiet Eastern front. The Allies were running out of troops, so they saw the American entry into the war as their needed source of reinforcements to continue the stalemate with Germany. However, Pershing shocked the Allied command by stating that he was determined that his troops would not be wasted in such a meaningless stalemate in the trenches.

Finally the British and French Prime Ministers called him to a private conference to personally pressure him into accepting their plan of using American troops as their reinforcements. The General shocked the Prime Ministers when he stood up, declared that he had already considered their plan and rejected it, and then walked out of the room leaving two of the most powerful men in the world sitting in stunned silence.

Pershing came to Europe for one reason—to win. He would not budge from his position, and the Allied command gave in to his plan, agreeing to let the Americans fight together as a separate force. While the American troops were being mobilized and trained, Pershing agreed to use some of them as temporary reinforcements for the British and French, but demanded that they be returned as soon as he called for them. This decision not only helped hold the lines while the American army was mobilizing, but it also gave many of the soldiers some badly needed battle experience.

When the Germans launched their long expected spring offensive, Pershing called for his dispersed troops, to the grief of the other Allies. The Americans quickly proved their mettle in battle, winning a series of notable victories that started to take the heat off the French and British lines. Pershing stunned the Germans by mounting a major offensive of his own, breaking through enemy lines in just two days, and causing the entire German offensive to grind to a halt.

Pershing did not lose time celebrating such a great victory. He pressed the attack, and positioned more than a half million men at the very enemy positions which the British and French had considered impregnable in the Argonne Forest. The battle raged for forty-seven days at a level of intensity almost unprecedented, even in this bloody war. More than 122,000 Americans fell, to the rising consternation of the nation, but still he pushed his troops forward. Finally the Americans broke through the most strategic point of the German defenses, and cut their lines of supply and communication. The Kaiser fled to Holland, and Germany surrendered only weeks after it seemed they were sure to win.

The American army suffered huge casualties for such a short period of time, but there were probably not nearly as many as they would have suffered in just a few months of trench warfare which could have prolonged the war indefinitely. Pershing understood this, and his refusal to fight trench warfare broke the stalemate and won the war.

None of the other Allied commanders had foreseen such a possibility for victory because the trenches had conditioned them. Pershing was a visionary, and he fought for one purpose—victory. He pressed the attack until he prevailed. Overall, the cost of his victory was far less than the casualties he would have paid if he had not been so bold.

To a great extent the victory in World War I must be attributed to the incredible endurance and sacrifice of the British and French forces. Pershing rightly honored them for what they had accomplished. However, for one who had been stalemated as a junior officer for so much of his life, when he got the chance to lead he was going to do it.

When the young and cocky lead, it is often to disaster. Courage is essential for leadership, but much more than just courage is needed for effective leadership that accomplishes its goal. Pershing went to battle for one reason—to defeat the enemy and win the war. This required courage, but also a wise strategy. He knew that the Argonne Forest was geographically the strongest point in the enemy's lines, but wise generals, such as the Germans had, would put their weakest troops in such places because that was where they were least likely to be attacked. Pershing knew his enemy and his own troops, and he saw an opportunity for victory where no one else would even look. Leadership must be willing to look beyond the present conditions, and beyond the obvious. Leadership must always look for the way to win.

CHAPTER SEVEN

FINDING YOUR PURPOSE

Getting a specific vision is crucial if we are going to succeed. However, our vision will often be general at first, and then get more specific as we proceed toward the goal. For example, you may fall in love with music at a young age and know that you want to devote your life to it. But it can be years before you are able to focus on that aspect of music for which you are truly gifted, such as playing a specific instrument, composing, etc. You may discover that your true love is for building things. As you start getting some experience in the construction trades, you may learn that you like commercial construction better than residential. Then you may find that you love engineering. In this way you zero in on your true love, which will almost always be where your true talent is found.

In this process we are often finding out and eliminating who we are *not*, as well as who we are. Because of this, many people who have left a mark on the world went through a process of what appeared to be failure before they became a success. Properly understood, many experiences that we may think were failures were just course changes toward our ultimate purpose. These course changes should be distinguished from the ones that we make out of opposition or obstacles.

Likewise, there are successes that may dictate a course change. Many achieve a goal only to learn that it was not the fulfillment they were expecting. We must view every day of our lives as a school that is meant to prepare us for where we are heading. Every explorer has gone up a few box canyons and had to retrace their steps before finding the path through. That is not wasted time. Part of every explorer's job is to map the territory so that those who come after them can avoid the box canyons. Those who leave their mark on the world do not just arrive at their destination; they make the way for everyone else to get there easier.

Even so, we must see that for us to achieve the place of ultimate effectiveness, we must see our path becoming straighter as we go. To accomplish what we are gifted to do, we must learn to refrain from that which we are not gifted to do. Knowing who we are *not* is part of the process of learning who we are.

In my own research, I have found that it is a very small percentage of people who actually work in the field in which they received their degree. Was their time in college wasted? Certainly most gain a lot from their education even if they do not work in their field of study, but how much more effective could our education be if we were more certain of our purpose before we start? Learning to identify our purpose is the first step toward fulfilling it, and we have not found it if we are not certain that we are touching the deepest desires of our heart. If we are going to be leaders, and accomplish anything of significance, we must come to know our own heart, and have the fortitude to follow it. We must also have the wisdom and maturity to be able to distinguish our true heart's devotion from just things that we like or even fantasies.

SPECIALIZATION IS GROWTH

Once we get on the right trail we can expect it to become even clearer as we walk it. One can look at the advance of civilization and see that advancement has followed the pattern of increasing specialization. That is why the development of the assembly line, where different individuals did just one part of the job instead of each trying to complete the whole product, multiplied productivity many times over. As the assembly line was perfected, ten individuals working together did not just multiply their productivity by ten, but by a thousand times. This development is now credited with changing civilization more than any other single factor, and thrusting us into the modern age.

Now, assembly line jobs may be more tedious, and we may be glad to see robots taking over most of them. That too is progress, but even if we are presently doing the most tedious, monotonous job, if we will do it like Michelangelo painted, we will start to find great fulfillment in it. Again, it is possible to find greatness and fulfillment in anything we do. If we do every job with that attitude, we will continue making upward progress toward even greater things.

Even a cursory view of the world reveals that the more jobs which have been broken down into speciality fields, the more effective each job has become and the faster that field has advanced. You can see this in industry, science, medicine, and even sports. Two hundred years ago the town barber was also the town surgeon. How many of us want to go back to that? Look how far surgery has come since they decided that it should become a specialty! Look at how much further it has come since the field of surgery began to specialize around the various organs of the body. If brain surgery is needed, you will have much more confidence in a neural surgeon than one who is a gifted plastic surgeon.

Basic biology teaches us that as soon as a living thing stops the process of growing, it begins the process of dying. Our goal must be continued advancement and growth which will almost always require continued specialization and focus.

Many years ago I heard a Cuban refugee who had just moved to Atlanta say, "I really appreciate those huge road signs that tell you which way to get to Interstate 85, but I appreciate even more those little signs that let you know that you are still on Interstate 85!" It is good to find out the general field to which we are called, or to see the big sign that tells us the way to the road we want to be on. However, it is also important to recognize the little signs along the way that let us know we are still on the right path. Again, a primary sign that we are still on the right path is for us to be growing in love with what we are doing.

The big sign that points to the path that you should be on will usually be a great love that is first felt for your vocation or venture. This love should point you in the right direction. Ancient mystics called this the "first love." This is what a man and woman first feel for one another that leads to marriage. However, love changes in a marriage. The great passion we know at first changes into something that may be less fiery but can become deeper and more fulfilling. A superficial person will sometimes view the lessening of the fiery passion of first love as a loss of love, but it is intended to be the beginning of an even deeper relationship.

The same is usually true of our vocation. The goal should not be to keep the first passion going but to keep on the path of love. If we stay on the path there will be times of great fiery passion, but we cannot expect that every day and we probably could not survive it if we did. Passion is just one aspect of love, and it is important, but the little signs along the way are just as crucial.

THE ESSENTIAL FACTOR

Faith is the primary factor that separates those who will accomplish their goals from those who do not. This is not just faith in God, but also faith in general. Everyone has faith; everyone believes *something*. There are principles of faith that will work for anyone who uses them, whether they believe in God or not. The faith we have will determine the course of our lives.

If we have faith in ourselves and our natural talents, then we will probably use them. If we have more faith in the obstacles before us than in the talents we have, those obstacles will dictate what we do or do not do. If we have more faith in our weaknesses than in our gifts, the weaknesses will probably prevail in our life and we will be perpetual failures. Faith is a basic determining force in our lives and it will be a primary determining factor of whether we succeed or fail.

You may or may not believe that Jesus was the Son of God, but what He accomplished was unprecedented in all of human history. He came from the most despised town in the most despised nation on earth. He then took some of the lowliest and most despised people in that nation and released a force in them that transformed the world to the degree that the very word "history" was derived from His-story. The force that He released in them was faith.

History testifies that there is no force on earth that can stop true faith. Jesus told His disciples that if they just had faith the size of a grain of mustard seed that they could move mountains. These disciples not only moved mountains, they moved nations and empires. They understood the principle of the seed. If even the seed could move mountains, what would the full plant do? Along with the knowledge of what you want to do, you must also have the faith to keep going until every obstacle is removed from your path. That is another goal of this book, to sow seeds of confidence that will grow, enabling you to proceed on your course with increasing boldness. You must have this to get where you're going.

Now we will move on to some of the more powerful principles of leadership that can enable us to begin creating our own futures.

CHAPTER EIGHT

LEADERSHIP THAT SHAPES THE WORLD

As we examine the principles of leadership in greater depth, I will also include a review of a few basic principles and examine some of the extraordinary ways in which they were used.

It was a firm grasp of basic leadership principles that enabled Napoleon, an obscure soldier from Corsica, to take a bankrupt and war devastated France and defeat the most powerful nations on earth, dominating Europe during his time. The great question of history has been, "Did Napoleon make the times or did the times make Napoleon?" When we understand leadership we will know that Napoleon made the times in which he lived. We will also realize that any soldier could arise and do the same thing.

Napoleon called himself "the little corporal" as a way to identify with his men. Hitler literally was a little corporal, was never commissioned as an officer and yet he arose to dominate some of the great generals of his time. For a while he dominated Europe even more than Napoleon had in the past. To do this he seized a few basic principles of leadership, and used them better than the generals and other politicians he dominated.

As stated, if the good do not use these principles, then evil men will. Hitler used them so well that even Churchill said that had Hitler died in 1938, he would have been considered one of the greatest leaders of all time. Let's look briefly at what he accomplished.

When Hitler came to power, Germany was one of the weakest and most impoverished nations in the world. More than 50 percent of the nation was unemployed. After the German mark fell to a value of several trillion to a dollar, it was finally declared worthless. The national debt was many times the Gross National Product and growing dramatically by the day. Gangs ruled whole cities and the German military was the weakest in Europe. In just four years Hitler not only restored the economy but made it the most powerful in Europe. He raised the employment to 100 percent. He did not just balance the budget in four years, (that alone would have seemed miraculous) but he paid off the national debt. He did this while also rebuilding the German military, establishing it as the most powerful in the world. Churchill was right. No one has ever done anything like this before or since.

Such accomplishments make it a little easier to understand why generals and even prime ministers of other nations were in awe of him, and tended to overlook the great and tragic darkness that was also present with his leadership.

On the other hand, it was by using principles of leadership that Gandhi, a humble lawyer from India, broke the strength and will of the greatest empire in the world at the time and gave birth to a nation. He did this without firing a shot and without holding a political office or military position. There are different ways to implement the principles of leadership. As we have established, one of the basic characteristics of leadership is that it is creative.

It was using basic principles of leadership combined with creativity in ways that had never been used in the battlefield before that enabled Robert E. Lee to take the hungry and poorly equipped Southern Army during the Civil War, and cause the world to stop and marvel as he won victory after victory against impossible odds.

Jesus was a carpenter, and he gathered a little band of ordinary and even lowly people, and released the greatest forces of change the world has ever experienced. He took these seemingly insignificant people and turned them into some of the most extraordinary examples of leadership ever produced. Two of His followers, Paul and Silas, after suffering continuous persecution and slander, without arms or bands of followers, caused the highest officials of the most powerful empire on earth to cringe with fear when they limped into a city, exclaiming, "Those who have turned the world upside down have now come here to us."

When finally captured, Paul penned a few letters from his prison cell—hardly a significant literary accomplishment. Even so, no other words have ever been reprinted as often, distributed as widely, or impacted the world as much as those brief letters that are now immortalized as canon Scripture.

All of these men used basic leadership principles. Leadership is a most powerful force to be entrusted to mere men. It affects our lives every day. Understanding leadership is fundamental to understanding the world we live in, and how we fit into it. If we understand it we can live beyond the ordinary and mundane in order to make a difference on this earth. If we do not understand it, we will always be subject to it.

As stated previously, leadership combines several characteristics to make one both perceptive and effective in accomplishing goals. The effective leader will not only have the vision to perceive the future; he will have the wisdom, courage, and determination to affect it. All human advancement is the result of leadership. Our own advancement will depend on the degree to which we embrace it.

LEADERSHIP VERSUS MANAGEMENT

To rightly use leadership we must distinguish it from management. Confusing management with leadership has caused many enterprises to fall short of their potential, and in many cases, to fail altogether. Both leadership and management are required for the administration of almost every venture, but they must be recognized as separate, and kept within their own spheres of authority.

The qualities that make a good leader will often make one a poor manager. The qualities that make a good manager can hinder one from becoming an effective leader. That is why having good leadership characteristics will not guarantee that one will be a *successful* leader. To be a successful leader one must know how to gather and employ good managers. Not recognizing this need for dependence upon those with different talents has caused some of the most brilliant leaders to briefly excite their world only to fizzle out quickly, having no foundation for lasting success.

Managers must be detail-oriented to be successful; leaders must be concept-oriented, able to see the big picture. Good leaders usually dislike details; good managers may have a hard time seeing beyond them. Of course there are exceptions to this. There are effective managers with leadership ability, and leaders with good management ability. However, the more undistracted devotion we can give to our strongest talents, the more effective we will be.

Being too involved with the details makes it hard to see the big picture. Likewise, when one is focused on the big picture it is hard to see the details effectively. The most effective leadership comes from a partnership of those who lead and those who manage, a partnership that allows each to concentrate on his or her own role.

Almost every great enterprise has been founded by a leader, not a manager. Even so, almost every enterprise that lives past its founder is then taken over by a manager. There are two basic reasons for this: 1) There are so few leaders who can make it through the gauntlet of the hierarchy, and 2) Most leaders are poor managers and fail to understand the need for a partnership with managers. Consequently, the enterprise will be in desperate need of a manager at the top after the leader's time.

When the manager first takes over, profitability and efficiency will usually increase for a period of time, but progress under the manager type will invariably be slow, jeopardizing future success. Then the organization will usually swing back to a leader-type for its next head. Most organizations, from corporations to churches that have existed for a period of time, will constantly switch from manager-type to leader-type at the top.

THE GAUNTLET

The advancement system in a typical hierarchy (which is the structure of almost every human enterprise) makes it hard for one with good leadership qualities to rise to a position of leadership. The lower echelons of a hierarchy usually reward management skills more than those of leadership. A leader will rarely be good enough at the managerial skills required for advancement within the system—unless he devotes himself to the quality that will be most needed when he does come to his place of leadership—*discipline*.

The leader must understand the detail-oriented management skills so foreign to his nature, if he is to effectively work with those whose work will be essential to his success as a leader. The typical hierarchy system will be most difficult for even a great leader to advance in, but those who do advance will be better prepared for their task. Even if it is tedious and boring, the potential leader should see the hierarchy as his cocoon. It is the great struggle required by the butterfly to get out of its cocoon that strengthens it so that it can use those huge wings. It will likewise be the potential leader's struggle to get to the top of the hierarchy which prepares him for the great responsibility of leadership.

THE ESSENTIAL PARTNERSHIP

Advancement requires seeing beyond the present limits of our time, a realm where the true leader abides, but where the manager has difficulty. A manager looks at what *is*; a leader is always looking for what *can be*. It takes both qualities to get the full picture required for success. One without the other is ultimately doomed to mediocrity or failure. If the managers understood leadership, and the leaders understood management, there would almost certainly be far less of a decline in enterprise, and both leadership and management would be more effective.

The leader's job is to give the managers direction, vision, and inspiration. Regardless of how good the leader is, he will be ineffective without good managers. His degree of success or failure will be determined by the quality of managers he can recruit. Discerning the quality and ability of his people and using them properly is just as important in accomplishing goals as having the vision and other resources required for the enterprise.

General Robert E. Lee is considered one of the great military leaders of all time. General "Stonewall" Jackson and General James Longstreet were two great military managers. As *a team,* they may have been as close to being invincible as any two generals ever came. It was a simple coalition; Lee would determine what needed to be done, Jackson and Longstreet would determine how to do it.

Most likely none of these celebrated generals without the other would have ever risen to the heights of accomplishment that they were able to attain as a team. With Jackson and Longstreet to take the burden of management, Lee could concentrate on what he did best—seeing the overall picture. Without Lee being so willing to delegate, the abilities of Jackson and Longstreet to implement these strategies may have gone unnoticed or under used. Working as a team made each of them great, while giving each the opportunity to realize their full potential. Such teams are rare, but would probably be more common if we just had the insight to see and give opportunity to the qualities and potential of our co-workers.

Lee was also a very good military manager, and Jackson was certainly an outstanding leader. These abilities are not always mutually exclusive, but most leaders who have achieved success did so with the support of talented managers who enabled them to concentrate on the big picture. Although exceptions to this are rare, two of the most notable leaders in history remarkably lived during the same period, and actually confronted each other in one of the great epic military battles of all time—Napoleon and Wellington who faced each other at The Battle of Waterloo.

Napoleon was a colossus, the type of leader who has only emerged once every few hundred years. He was not only a great military genius, but also a great political genius. It was this combination that enabled him to dominate the age in which he lived, and to a large degree, set the course of history since his time. Some of his military innovations would provide a foundation for modern military strategy. Some of his political innovations have done the same for government and law.

MANAGEMENT BASED LEADERSHIP

Napoleon's genius for military strategy was actually based on a profound understanding and use of military management. Likewise, his genius for political leadership was born out of his deep understanding of political management. Napoleon is a study of how this rare combination of great leadership and great management can carry one to the very limits of human potential. The few leaders who have been so gifted have dominated almost every great period in history.

Napoleon's innovative military strategies were based on the maneuverability of his forces. This maneuverability was based upon his management strategies, which streamlined the method of supplying the troops. This opened strategic possibilities for Napoleon that the opposing forces did not even have the option of considering. In simplistic terms, those who "get there first with the most" usually achieve military victory. Because of this he could so outmaneuver a superior force that Napoleon was able to use a single army to rout several others in quick succession.

Except for Wellington, it could be argued that Napoleon had no peer in history on the field of battle. But Wellington was not only his peer; he was arguably a better military leader *and* manager than Napoleon, though he was no match for Napoleon politically. Even so, possibly the only man in history who could stop Napoleon on the battlefield was the one who did stop him. The odds against two men as remarkable as Napoleon and Wellington living during the same period, much less actually confronting one another in battle, would defy computation. The battle itself, Waterloo, met or surpassed any expectations of the genius in management and power of leadership that these two brought to this confrontation.

Wellington was a British officer who began his military career in India. He gained some notoriety by winning battles and subduing forts with intelligence and innovation. Even so, this did not gain him much respect due to the low regard the public had for his adversaries. Through a remarkable set of circumstances, he was transferred and given command of The Peninsula Campaign in Portugal and Spain. While the depressed allies expected little out of this campaign, Wellington surprised the world by liberating Portugal and Spain, defeating some of Napoleon's top generals and troops.

Wellington's victories, combined with Napoleon's debacle in Russia, sent Napoleon into exile. With the armies disbanded, Wellington returned to Britain. Early the next year Napoleon returned to France, quickly gathered his loyal troops, and marched on Brussels. Wellington was dispatched to command a hastily assembled allied army comprised of diverse troops with different languages and bickering generals who were in some cases political appointees with little military ability. Few of his lieutenants understood Wellington's newly devised strategies. Because of these problems and the fact that he was facing possibly the greatest military genius of all time with a much smaller force, Wellington's task looked impossible. It was the setting for one of the great demonstrations of military leadership of all time.

PEACE OF MIND—A FOUNDATION FOR VICTORY

How can anyone feel at peace in the midst of a battle? Wellington's calm in battle had become as legendary as his military innovations. On one occasion, after giving orders that he felt would accomplish the victory, he was seen catching a quick snooze right on the field of battle. The night before Waterloo, with Brussels in a panic, he actually attended a gala ball. A number of his victories were directly attributed to his personal entry into the thickest part of the battle to rally his troops, and he was never seen to flinch even as men fell all around him. Wellington acknowledged that his peace in the midst of such conflict was supernatural, a gift from above. At Waterloo, supernatural leadership and supernatural management would also be required of him.

Just south of Brussels, one hundred and fifty thousand men faced each other in less than three square miles of territory. Napoleon had nothing but contempt for "the sepoy general" he faced that day. He seemed almost bored with the looming battle, and was looking forward to dining in Brussels that evening.

ARROGANCE—THE FOUNDATION FOR DEFEAT

Besides scorn for his adversary's ability, Napoleon knew he had significant numerical advantages in troops and guns. He even slept late, almost casually arraying his troops and did not begin the battle until after eleven o'clock. This poor timing was possibly the only strategic mistake Napoleon was to make that day, but it was all that Wellington would need.

A biblical proverb states, "Pride comes before the fall," and that explains the downfall of many of history's great leaders. At Waterloo, Napoleon gave one of history's most resounding punctuations to that truth. Previous successes can be the seed of ultimate destruction if they produce arrogance.

With the sun already high, Napoleon ordered his artillery to begin one of the greatest cannonades ever witnessed. Then a huge thunderstorm broke upon the field that actually drowned out the cannonade, disconcerting the French. (This thunderstorm phenomenon had accompanied some of Wellington's most important victories. He called them "the finger of God.") The deluge so softened the field that the cannon balls lost some of their deadly potential as the ground just absorbed them. The mud also reduced Napoleon's maneuverability. This was just the beginning of a score of "miracles" Wellington would need, and receive that day. But it was not *just* the miracles that saved him; he was a man who was prepared to brilliantly seize and derive every drop of help that he could from each one.

CRISIS—THE COCOON OF THE GREAT

All day long the wounded and routed allied soldiers poured into Brussels. Every new group gave the same report—Wellington was beaten and the French were just behind them. Actually their reports were understandable. At any time during the day one could have looked at the allied position and determined that it was hopeless. One general later reported, "From noon until the very last moment of the battle, it was one continuous crisis."

It was under just such pressure that Wellington excelled. He seemed to be omnipresent. He was always at the point of the greatest crisis, directing and rallying his men. He kept the big picture of the overall battle while he also personally directed individual regiments. He kept track of every "pawn" in this most deadly chess match. He seemed to always appear just in time, with just enough men, and with just enough resolve to barely escape disaster. After plugging one hole he would gallop off to the other end of the field where he suspected another emergency, and he would usually find it as expected. A lesser man would have retreated or surrendered a dozen times that day. Napoleon brilliantly pressed every advantage but was repeatedly stopped by the narrowest of margins.

By mid-afternoon Napoleon began to suspect that "the sepoy general" had some ability. That morning Napoleon had told his staff that the odds were ten to one that they would be in Brussels by nightfall. By afternoon he acknowledged to those gathered around him that the odds were now only three to two.

Finally Napoleon's General Ney overwhelmed the outnumbered allies to take strategic ground in the center of Wellington's position. This was the most feared disaster for the allies. Napoleon astutely followed up this advantage with what would certainly be the death blow—he sent his famous Old Guard into the gaping hole in Wellington's center.

In their many battles, the Guard had never been repulsed. Both armies stood in awe at their massive assault in parade formations across the field. Wellington may have been the only one on the entire field who gave himself a chance at that point. Amazingly, he was observed as confident and calm as ever. A cannon shot sailed over the neck of his horse and cleanly severed the leg of his second in command. Wellington simply reached over and shook the general's hand, expressing his condolences, and galloped off to another vantage point.

As the Guard approached Wellington's center, he waved his hand, and a regiment rose from behind a stonewall to pour a deadly volley into the French. Then out of a cornfield emerged Colonel Colborne's regiment. Colborne's general galloped up to him to ask his intentions. Colborne stated simply, "I'm going to make that column feel my fire." At that moment Wellington's aide arrived with the order for Colborne to advance from the cornfield.

All day long Wellington had remarkably kept in his mind the position of every brigade and regiment. In spite of the multitude of crises in which he could have desperately used this regiment, he resisted until the *perfect* time.

The battle for the center became a caldron of death. The Old Guard felt Colborne's fire and they faltered. At this point, Colborne heard a voice beside him saying, "Go ahead, press them. You're doing it, press them now." The colonel turned to see who was speaking and was astonished to find Wellington himself.

The entire French army groaned as they beheld a sight they had never witnessed before—the Guard's perfect formations disintegrating as they fled from their positions in disarray. After being pressed to the limits all day, Wellington's most desperate crisis quickly became his one brief opportunity for victory—and he seized it. He poured his few remaining reserves into the fray, and at the right time the Belgian division arrived.

Moments before, the situation had appeared completely hopeless, then the entire French army began to collapse. The Guard's reserves formed squares and took their stand to protect the retreat. After they were surrounded, and were asked to surrender, their reply was to the point: "The Old Guard dies, but it never surrenders." They died and Napoleon's power over Europe died with them.

As darkness fell, more than fifty thousand men lay upon the field. More than a dozen men had attended Wellington that morning; that evening he dined with his one remaining aide. He felt no elation in the victory. In keeping with his notorious understatements concerning his own accomplishments, he simply claimed to have done what anyone else would have done in his place. This tendency was never given or perceived as a false modesty; Wellington was a remarkably humble man. If he ever succumbed to overstatement it was in relation to his shortcomings, not his accomplishments. The truly great do not have to blow their own trumpets—others will do it for them.

Napoleon was defeated by his own arrogance. Wellington was confident but never arrogant. This is a difference that every truly great leader has understood. Effective confidence is founded in a humility that produces a right perspective of his circumstances. Wellington's belief in his appointed destiny gave him the ability to keep peace of mind under the greatest of pressures. It is possible that no other man in history ever faced such pressure from crisis after crisis within a single day, with so much at stake, and yet performed so brilliantly. Even the smallest mistake, or slightest hesitancy in reacting to any single one of the crises could have meant doom, not only for his army, but also for Europe.

The real test of leadership always comes in a crisis, and there will be crises for everyone in leadership. Almost every businessperson will sooner or later have to make decisions that can mean life or death to his business. Often, the more successful the businessperson, the more frequent such decisions will have to be made. The greater the potential for success inherent in the decision, the greater the potential for failure it will likewise carry.

Every coach will have to call plays that mean victory or defeat. The more successful the coach, the more such calls he or she will have to make, and the higher the stakes will be. It may not be too difficult to make the proper decision or to call the right play when there is little on the line. The difference between the great ones and the rest is the ability to do it in the crisis when there is more at risk.

DEFEAT—THE FOUNDATION FOR FUTURE VICTORY

I once built a successful business in a short period of time. To build it as rapidly as I did, I had to make dozens of decisions that could have meant life or death to the venture. I made many right decisions that paid great dividends. I then made just one bad decision, and that single mistake ultimately led to the bankruptcy of the entire business. It was a painful, humiliating failure, but I consider it one of my most valuable experiences. I learned more from that one defeat than from all of my victories combined.

The baseball player who stands at the plate with the potential for being the hero can also be the goat. Just as Wellington turned the biggest reversal of the day into his chance for victory, we must maintain the same resolve. By maintaining patience and peace of mind in the midst of a crisis, you will usually see an opportunity to use the situation to your advantage.

The 1980s saw the amazing rise of the Christian *mega ministries*. It was no surprise that such ministries which grew so fast would stay in a perpetual state of crisis, tottering between oblivion and extraordinary advancement. After overcoming a multitude of life and death struggles, some of the biggest and most successful of these ministries began to unravel because of just one major mistake by their leaders. The lessons abound that one moment of weakness and poor judgment is able to undo many years of labor built upon good judgment and effective leadership in crisis. However, if you want to play the game for the big stakes, those are the rules.

With success comes power, and power inevitably brings a subtle corruption of our judgment—a perceived invincibility that is often a fatal delusion. One of the most important ingredients of Wellington's character was his ability to have confidence while not thinking more highly of himself than he should. The apostle Paul in his letters penned from prison, gave a most appropriate warning to those in leadership, "When you think you stand, take heed lest you fall." This illusion of invincibility could be called *The Titanic Syndrome*.

CHAPTER NINE

THE TITANIC SYNDROME

When it was built, the Titanic was a symbol of the opulence and also the sense of invincibility felt by the British Empire in those days. She reflected that period's extravagance, and arrogance, as well as the belief that nothing could sink its expanding world economy and dominion. Few at that time dreamed that in just two years the world would be at war, and their invincible empire was about to hit an iceberg that would ultimately send it to the same end as all of man's previous empires.

The world's wealthy and famous streamed onto the Titanic for the maiden voyage. Because they didn't think she could sink, they sailed boldly into dangerous waters with reckless abandon. This "unsinkable" pride of the Empire proved to be incredibly fragile—just as the Empire was, as is every empire. Arrogance can be the greatest weakness of all.

In relation to the present world economy, it has been repeated often, and believed by most, that what happened in 1929 could never happen again. Experts say there are too many safeguards—a stronger Federal Reserve, higher margin requirements for speculators and institutions, FDIC, FSLIC, SIPC, etc. Do not believe it for a minute! We are as vulnerable now to a worldwide economic catastrophe as at any time in history. Pride will allow us to merrily sail along in the most treacherous of seas.

LEADERSHIP, THE POWER OF A CREATIVE LIFE

In 1929, United States corporations had $1.54 in cash for every $1.00 of debt. Presently, they have around $.15 in cash for each $1.00 of debt. If we start measuring individual and third world debt, not to mention the still present huge federal debt, the economic icebergs in our path begin to seem completely impassable.

The Federal Reserve, FDIC and all the other safeguards are lifeboats that may save a few, but they are wholly inadequate to save the whole economy if we hit serious misfortune. The owners of the Titanic felt that carrying even half the lifeboats for a ship of her size, was superfluous; after all, she was unsinkable! Today's leaders are sailing with the same disdain, while touting their ingenuity in designing a ship they think cannot sink. We must not let the euphoria of such things as the collapsing of communism cause us to succumb to the terrible delusion that we do not always need to have the humility that will keep us vigilant.

Democracy is the most just and benevolent form of government devised by man, but it is by no means the most efficient. Its nature makes it difficult for leaders to face problems until they have become a crisis. Because of the process required for election in a democracy, those who are best qualified to either lead or manage seldom get involved. Historically we have been blessed with enough leadership that was just in time to save us from oblivion when crisis exploded upon us. Even so, an ever present potential for financial crisis can be the most deadly we have ever confronted.

When the Titanic hit the iceberg, there was a disconcerting jolt. Just about everyone noticed it, but after a few seconds the party continued. From the captain to the last third class passenger, no one imagined that in just a couple of hours most of them would be on the bottom of the sea. The ship was so big and warm, and all the "experts" said that it was unsinkable. It was not the iceberg that sank the Titanic—it was *COMPLACENCY.* Wise and decisive leadership could have prevented the disaster, and it can prevent future disasters for us.

Historians marvel at the repetitious cycles of human error. Few have been able to break out of these cycles. Few have been wise enough to see anything but what they wanted to see in the trends and events taking place around them. Those in authority, by the nature of their power, feel compelled to put the best face on problems. Only the most courageous leaders have been able to hear the warnings and take action. Empire after empire, nation after nation, companies, organizations, churches, and families continue to fail because their leaders refuse to face problems until they are beyond control.

Roger Smith, the former Chairman of General Motors, stated after the October 19, 1987 Stock Market crash, "We didn't just have a tummy ache here in our country; we had a genuine, certified heart attack! If you don't recognize it as a heart attack, and if you don't get on that diet and start doing your exercises, you can have another one and it could be terminal." In many ways this warning was heard, and a number of courageous changes have been made. However, once you have had a heart attack, you should never again let your guard down or another one will be much more likely.

In some ways, the economy parallels the operation of an engine and is often referred to as one. As a jet pilot one of the first things I learned was to pay attention to my engine instruments and know what they were telling me. Even if the particular systems were staying within their tolerances, certain trends could foretell serious problems. If there are erratic oscillations, even though they stay within given parameters, the engine may not just quit, it could very well explode! The economic instruments of the entire world have been oscillating. Even though they may at this time be within safe parameters, the continued oscillations are a sign that we must understand.

The degree of complacency of the leadership on the Titanic was incomprehensible and clearly the reason for the disaster. Captain Smith and his crew received numerous warnings about the ice field which lay directly across their path—and they did not even slow down! Even if she were unsinkable, to hit an iceberg head on would cause great damage and probably loss of life. But Smith ignored the danger while maintaining an incredible false sense of security. He wanted to break the record for passage to New York. When looking at the course of Western economic policy for the last few decades some of the parallels are striking. There is a mad race to break all records, to keep pushing ahead at a dangerous pace.

As the recent economic advance has continued for several years, I have watched a most disconcerting kind of complacency grow—that is the lack of appreciation for the jobs and prosperity that we have. The quality of workmanship in many trades has measurably fallen. Workers have become increasingly callous toward complaints because they know they can always find another job, or another customer. The ultimate, true value of our economy is tied directly to the quality of our products. It seems now that a recession could be one of the healthiest things that could happen to jolt us back to reality, and true value back into what we have been so blessed with.

As the Titanic sailed merrily along, her crew had never held a proper lifeboat drill. They had no plan for the orderly movement of passengers to the boats, and most of the crew did not even know how to lower them. Everything had to be planned and learned while the ship was sinking under their feet which contributed to a much greater loss of life than was necessary. Many boats were lowered only partially filled, one with just twelve people while the crew held hundreds of passengers below the deck. The entire ship had been caught off guard by the events of that fateful night and they paid dearly for it.

Will we be caught in the same way? If we are, we will pay just as dearly. The ability to cope with a crisis is necessary for anyone in leadership, but an even higher goal is to have enough wisdom to take action *before* the situation reaches a crisis. How many of our crises are unnecessary and are actually the result of poor leadership?

THE LEADERS

There were two other ships that played a significant role in the drama of the Titanic disaster: the Californian and the Carpathia. The captains of these ships, along with Smith of the Titanic, reflect some of the best and the worst characteristics of leadership.

The Californian had a reserved and cautious captain. When he heard about the ice in his path, he slowed down. When he saw the ice, he ordered the ship stopped and waited for daylight. His wireless (radio) operator began warning the other ships in the area of the danger. At 7:30 p.m. her warning was received and logged by the Titanic.

This was one of six warnings the Titanic received that evening, all of which were disregarded. This as much as anything tells the story of the indifference that permeated her bridge. It was not just the captain, but also the entire bridge staff who received and paid little or no attention to the warnings. When this attitude overcomes the leadership, doom is imminent.

The usually stormy North Atlantic was amazingly calm that night. More than one officer said they had never seen the sea so tranquil. First officer Lightoller of the Titanic made this observation at the inquiry when he declared: "everything was against us."

The tranquility of the sea must have also overcome the crew of the Californian. Her bridge watch saw the Titanic approaching just a few miles away; then they saw her stop dead in the water. At first they thought she was taking the same precautions for the ice that they had taken. The captain told the watch to wake him if there were any developments. Then the Titanic fired a rocket, which is always a distress signal at sea. When awakened the captain reasoned that she must have been signaling another company ship that they could not see. The wireless operator was asleep and they did not even wake him to see if he could contact the Titanic. Then more rockets were fired as the Californian's crew continued to delude themselves with the same explanation. They actually watched the Titanic go down, telling each other as her lights dimmed and slipped beneath the sea that she was sailing away! Had they responded to the first distress signal, the Californian may well have been able to save all of those who perished.

The complacency on the Titanic and the Californian may seem beyond belief, but will the present political and economic leadership look any less frozen in their stupor to the next generation? When the final inquiry comes and the story is told, are we going to be facing the same judgment? Will the band keep playing for us while we slip beneath the sea? Rationalization is a popular shield for cowards while those with the courage to proclaim the warning are dubbed "alarmists," and their message negativism.

The other ship in the fateful drama of the Titanic was the Carpathia, captained by Arthur H. Rostron. He was known for his ability to make quick decisions and to energize those who served under him. He was a pious man devoted to prayer. At 12:35 a.m. the Carpathia's wireless operator burst into Rostron's quarters to report that the Titanic had struck an iceberg. Rostron reacted in character—he immediately ordered the Carpathia to turn around and accelerate to full speed in the direction of the Titanic; then he asked the wireless operator if he was sure of the message! This showed a remarkable contrast to the reaction of the Californian crew.

Rostron then gave a powerful demonstration of truly prepared leadership—he thought of everything. He ordered the English doctor to the first class dining room, the Italian doctor to second class, the Hungarian to third class, along with every possible piece of equipment or supplies needed for sick or injured. He ordered different officers to different gangways, instructing them to get the names of survivors to send by wireless. They prepared block and lines with chair slings for the injured. Bowlines were secured along the sides of the ship, with boat ropes and heaving lines for securing the lifeboats. All gangway doors were opened. He directed specific officers to be in charge of his present passengers, to take care of their needs and keep them out of the way. All hands were ordered to prepare coffee, soup, and provisions. He designated the officer's cabins, smoke rooms, library, etc. to accommodate the survivors. Stewards were sent to reassure and explain the activity to their own passengers.

Then Rostron turned to face the biggest problem of all—the ice. He was heading at full speed into the same field that the Titanic had hit. To him reducing speed was out of the question, but he took every measure to reduce the risk to his own ship and passengers. He added a man to the crow's nest, put two more on the bow, one on each wing of the bridge, and he stayed there himself. His second officer, James Bisset, then noticed the captain taking one last measure that he considered the most important of all—he prayed.

At 2:45 a.m. Bisset saw the first iceberg. They steered around it and kept going. During the next hour they dodged five more. At 4:00 a.m. they reached the Titanic's last called position and began picking up lifeboats. As the sun rose, it revealed a sight they would never forget—the sea was full of icebergs for as far as the eye could see. Even with all the lookouts the Carpathia had passed numerous ones that they had not even seen.

The difficult rescue of the Titanic's survivors was carried out with such order that peace reigned over all. The Carpathia's passengers caught the spirit of self-sacrifice from the crew. Her first class passengers gave their own quarters to survivors; others did all they could. On one of the darkest nights of tragedy ever experienced on the high seas, the Carpathia's captain, crew, and passengers stand out as bright lights of courage and heroism. They are a demonstration of what true leadership is all about. They did not sleep as others did, and were not fooled by the calmness of the sea—they were prepared and they took action.

SUMMARY

To have a point of reference, I have used this message to relate to potential economic problems, but the lessons we can draw from it can be applied to any crisis. Pride and/or complacency can lead to a tragedy in any venture. Preparedness can enable us to confront any tragedy and save that which would otherwise be lost.

Wise leadership can keep us out of many crises. However, there are some that will come our way regardless of how wise or vigilant we are. There are too many factors in this world that we cannot control for us to ever be completely safe from them. It is right to try to avoid them, but also right to always be ready for them. The wise learn from the mistakes of others. The Titanic catastrophe probably has saved many other ships from a similar fate. It can also save ours if we will learn from it.

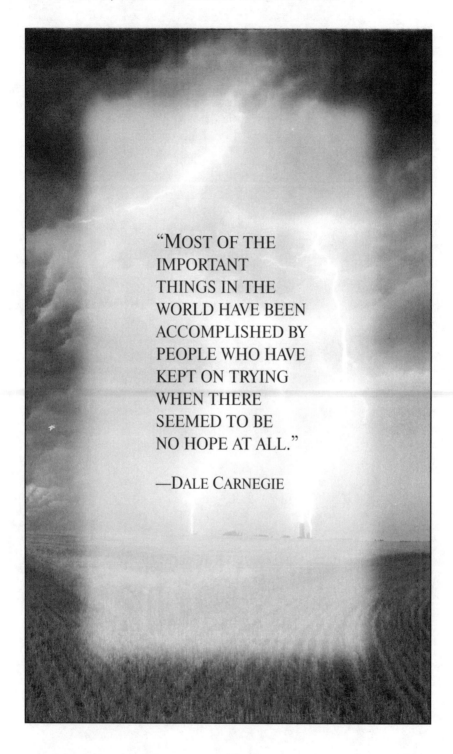

"MOST OF THE IMPORTANT THINGS IN THE WORLD HAVE BEEN ACCOMPLISHED BY PEOPLE WHO HAVE KEPT ON TRYING WHEN THERE SEEMED TO BE NO HOPE AT ALL."

—DALE CARNEGIE

CHAPTER TEN

SEEING THE FUTURE

In a classic book on leadership, *Hope is not a Method*, former Army Chief of Staff, Gordon R. Sullivan, and Michael V. Harper reveal a remarkable story about Lieutenant Colonel Hal Moore, which occurred during the Vietnam War. He commanded the 1st Battalion, 7th Cavalry in the central highlands of Vietnam in 1965. Advancing into a communist stronghold, his unit was quickly surrounded by forces that outnumbered them four or five to one. After four days of intense fighting, more than half of Moore's men were dead, but much heavier casualties had been inflicted on their enemies. Moore's men held their ground. Because this was the first pitched battle between the United States and North Vietnamese troops, it was considered a major test of performance in the growing conflict, which drew attention from the highest levels.

During the debriefing of Moore's men, an issue arose that alarmed the United States generals. At different times during the battle Moore was observed withdrawing into himself, seemingly shutting down and blocking out those around him. He was asked to explain this behavior while in danger of being overrun by the enemy. His answer not only satisfied his superiors that he was not being negligent but is now considered a basic procedure for commanders in battle. What was he doing?

The colonel related that he was trying to tune out all distractions so that he could answer three questions:

What is happening?

What is not happening?

What could he do to affect what was happening?

These are now considered the "three critical questions." If we would do whatever withdrawing is necessary to ask them on a regular basis, it is likely that our effectiveness in leadership would increase dramatically. If we are going to be effective leaders we must have a basis for understanding the present and determining what we can do about the future. This chapter is about gathering the knowledge required to do this. In the next chapter, we will look at how we can take that knowledge to create the future.

KNOW THE PAST, UNDERSTAND THE PRESENT, AND SEE THE FUTURE

A primary job of a leader is to discern the present, and to see the future. We will not lead successfully unless we know where we are going. We will not discern the present or see the future with perfect accuracy. However, to the degree we can see it, we will be able to plan a strategy that will impact the future as desired. Only then can a leader communicate the plan to those they are leading in a way that instills both the trust and resolve that will accomplish the desired outcome.

Evaluating the future requires analysis of both the past and present to identify trends. That is what Lieutenant Colonel Moore was trying to do. If he knew what was happening, he could analyze how best to respond to it with the resources available to him. He also needed to know what was *not* happening so that he would not waste valuable resources. In this way he was able to be pro-active and created the future he wanted.

Most of us have gone to a large shopping mall looking for a particular store. If you are unfamiliar with the mall you may try to find the map that tells where all the stores are located. However, that map will not do you much good without the little arrow that says, "You are here." That is the reference point. No map will do us much good unless we know where we are located on the map. Along with the question, "What is happening?" we also need to ask, "Where are we?"

There are some trends that we can see unfolding throughout recorded history. This may be a big map or panorama but the bigger, stronger, and deeper a foundation is, the greater its capacity to be built upon. The same is true of our knowledge. For this reason we will look briefly at the four major epochs of human history, and how they each affect us in the present. As we understand the big picture, it will be easier to understand our own time and the present trends. Then we will begin to understand more about how we can use these trends to our advantage, instead of uselessly resisting them.

THE FOUR POWERS OF CIVILIZATION

There have been four great epochs of human history that have each been built upon four great powers, and have affected humanity on a civilization wide basis. These four powers are:

1. Military

2. Religion

3. Politics

4. Economics

We can see that the first great historical epoch was dominated by military power. This was the age of the conquerors and great military empires such as Egypt, China, Babylon, Mongolia, Persia, Greece, and Rome. These empires were all built predominantly on military power.

The second great civilizational epoch was dominated by religion. This is religion as an institutional and social power, which should be distinguished from individual religious faith. During this period, the military power became a servant to the emerging religious powers such as Islam in the Middle East, Hinduism in the Far East, and Catholicism and Protestantism in the West. This period began to emerge around 300 A.D. and reached its peak during the Crusades and the great Ottoman Empire from about 1050 to 1500 A.D. During this period, the religious leaders were the most powerful men in the world. Most wars were religious conflicts, with the goal of conquering others for the sake of a religion, not just conquest for its own sake.

The next great civilizational epoch was dominated by politics. This period began during the 1500s and continued through the mid-twentieth century. This was the time of great political changes, when new forms of government were born through social upheavals such as the French, American, and Bolshevik revolutions. During this period both the religious and military powers became subservient to political powers. There were still religious and military wars, but the great sweeping social changes of this time were almost all political in nature and most of the wars were political in origin.

The transitional times between these great epochs were general, sometimes taking hundreds of years. About the beginning of the twentieth century we began to shift into a whole new epoch dominated by economic power. For example, the Bolshevik Revolution was both a political and an economic revolution, marking the beginning of this great shift in power centers. World War II was also a political and economic war. The Nazis would never have come to power without the oppressive and humiliating economic stranglehold imposed on Germany by the Versailles Treaty. Also, Japan attacked the United States in retaliation for economic sanctions which Japan called "an act of war."

When writing in the early eighteen hundreds, Clauswitz stated that war was the attempt of one nation to assert its political will over another nation. That was generally true for his time because he lived in the political age. If he had written this a few centuries before he would have probably stated that war was an attempt of one group to assert its religious will on another group. If he wrote this now he would probably say that war was the attempt of one nation to assert its economic will over another.

We are in the time when the primary motivating power in the world is economic. However, the foundations of military, religious, and political power are still with us, and still have significant influence. In some parts of the world, such as the Middle East, religion can still be a primary motivating power, but without question political and economic interests are mixed in, and sometimes even dominant. In Asia conflicts can still be political or religious, but they are primarily economic conflicts that use the other powers as motivating factors for the populace. Everywhere we now have at least some combination of these four great powers asserting the dominant influence. This is a paradigm that we can use to help us better understand a region or a people group.

This paradigm can also help us to understand events better, and how we might be able to affect them. The "Cold War" was a very real war, but it was an "economic" war. The real generals in this war were bank presidents and business leaders. The weapons were everything from consumer products to monetary exchange rates and stock markets. Even so, political changes wrought by these weapons were as great as the changes that have been made as the result of any military war in history.

The monetary crisis in Europe over a decade ago was the economic equivalent of a great military battle. It had to be fought before the European Union really had a chance to succeed. Instead of being fought with troops and artillery, it was fought with banks and currencies. We are now in the time when the military, religious, and political powers will be increasingly subservient to the economic powers. This is not to imply that this is right or wrong, but simply that it is so.

DEVELOPING YOUR OWN CIA

Like it or not, if you are a leader in any organization you are at war. Even if you are the leader of a charity, your enemy may be something as general as poverty, ignorance, or a specific disease. But to win your war you will have to mobilize, position your forces to your greatest advantage, and fight to win.

Most wars have been decided by one force gaining superior knowledge of its foe. This includes knowing its strengths, weaknesses, nature, common operating procedures, or intentions. Therefore, an effective and accurate intelligence gathering ability is crucial for an organization to succeed. You must know the strength and disposition of the forces opposing you, as well as the strength and disposition of your own resources.

The great Civil War General, Ulysses S. Grant, won his first significant battle at Fort Donaldson because he knew the opposing general so well from West Point. Grant knew him to be nervous and indecisive. Even though Grant was at a very dangerous disadvantage in many ways, including his position, troops, and weapons, he pressed the battle because he knew this was his foe's weakness. By being decisive, Grant convinced his foe that they were in fact in an impossible situation. They surrendered to him when they could have very easily destroyed Grant's army if there had been decisive leadership.

Having a good understanding of the ground we are on, and the forces opposing us, can go a long way toward achieving ultimate victory. The more we know about our situation, the more decisive we can be. Decisiveness will almost always be necessary for ultimate victory in any endeavor. However, decisiveness can almost never be dependent on perfect circumstances. We may at times be in as much darkness as our opposition but the one who takes the initiative first will usually win.

FOCUS OUR INTELLIGENCE GATHERING

It is good to have a general knowledge of major trends, but then we must narrow this information down to our own realm of activity. For example, coaches do not need to know too much about political trends unless it will affect their recruiting. They need to know the strengths and weaknesses of their own team as well as the same knowledge of opposing teams. Their intelligence gathering sources may include films of the previous games played by their opponents. They may use scouts who go to those games to bring back insights about the strengths and weaknesses of that team and their leadership. This information will be crucial for developing a game plan that will be successful.

A business leader will not only have to know his or her competition, but also market trends. Sources may be business news programs, periodicals, papers such as *The Wall Street Journal*, and even brokerage house research on individual businesses or industries. Of course, with billions of dollars potentially at stake, industrial spying is also becoming increasingly common.

With the accelerating pace of change, information is now considered the most valuable commodity. We must have information to understand the conditions and forces out there, and how they can impact future trends. We then need to know what our own resources are and how they can be used to bring about desired results.

There are many outside factors that can have a significant impact on business trends. These include politics, weather, geological, and even spiritual movements. We must determine the degree to which any of these can affect our organization, the degree to which we can affect them, and determine how much time and effort we will devote to intelligence gathering about them. We must learn to resist spending most of our time studying factors that have little or no impact on us, or that we can have little ability to impact. We want to devote our efforts to that which will make a significant difference.

WATCH THE PRIMARY POWERS

When we discern the sources of power that can affect our organization, or that we can affect, we need to keep our attention on them so that we can foresee trends. The Presidency of the United States is a primary center for military, political, and economic power. When candidate Reagan ran on a platform of strengthening the military, and tax cuts, it was easy to foresee what businesses would benefit from his victory at the polls. When it became obvious that he would win, wise business leaders were preparing for what was sure to come. Likewise, when a government begins to emphasize certain social programs, there will likely be beneficiaries in specific industries, and the wise will be ready for them.

After President Bush had led a remarkable political coalition to win the Persian Gulf War with unprecedented effectiveness, many people felt that he would be unbeatable in the next election. However, as impressive as his victory was in the political and military arena, this age is now dominated by economics. Bill Clinton brilliantly seized the initiative by building his whole campaign around the dominant power center of the present, not the past, and he won. Your heart may be in politics, or religion, but wise candidates today build their campaigns on economics.

Weather is not one of the powers that we can control, but it can have an obvious and significant impact on business trends. Hurricane Hugo destroyed a billion dollars worth of timber in South Carolina. Immediately, wise builders started preparing for the effect that this would have on them. Hurricane Andrew significantly changed building codes, not only in Florida, but also along the east coast. There were wise business leaders preparing for this the day after it struck. Droughts can have a great impact on food prices, but they can also be important factors in determining where certain businesses should be located. Geological factors can be just as important to analyze.

Even though religion is not the dominant power of this age, it is still having a profound impact on the world. Spiritual movements have the ability to greatly affect business trends, and overall these have had the biggest and most long lasting impact of all.

During the 1400s, the Reformation in Europe did much more than reform the church. Because of its emphasis on the faith of individuals rather than devotion to the institution of the church, this movement gave unprecedented value to the individual. This in turn gave birth to both democracy and the modern system of free enterprise, setting the stage for the Industrial Revolution, and the general course of business for the next five hundred years.

Of course, few are going to be concerned with predicting five hundred year trends. However, the further ahead we can see, the more effectively we are going to be able to prepare for and manage the immediate future.

There are obvious worldwide trends toward democracy, increasing liberty, and non-institutional Christianity. The dominance of institutional Christianity usually results in continued dominance by the ruling class. The spread of non-institutional Christianity has almost always resulted in increasing liberty and democracy as well as economic prosperity.

Until the Reformation, the largest consumer base consisted of the aristocracy, the church, and merchant class. This included a very small percentage of the population. As the common people gained rights, they gained power and wealth. The common class quickly became the largest consumer market. This kind of increasing demand for consumer products resulted in the industrial revolution and the development of assembly line production. Those who understood these trends and took the initiative required to take advantage of them quickly, acquired wealth at a pace and magnitude that before had only been available to sovereigns of nations.

The Reformation set off changes in politics and economics that were unprecedented in history. The first "Great Awakening" in America during the mid-1700s, and the second in the mid-1800s can be seen as the root of both the American Revolution and the American Civil War. Both raised demands for increased liberty, the first for the nation, and the second for slaves. These "Great Awakenings" were both the dominant political and economic forces during their time and had a huge affect on the future of the nation.

Smaller "revivals" such as the one sparked by the evangelist Sam Jones in Nashville in the late 1800s changed the economy of a large section of Tennessee and the surrounding states. At the time, Nashville was a center of gambling, distilling, and prostitution. Riverboats that had been floating casinos were soon carrying spiritual pilgrims from different parts of the country to the revival. They brought singing and a convergence of styles, which gave birth to new musical styles. Soon Nashville became known as "Music City." Large church denominations also moved their headquarters there. This spawned publishing as well as music production companies. As the drinking and gambling were reduced, productivity increased, drawing other businesses and industries.

Asia, Africa, South and Central America are presently experiencing the growth of basic, non-institutional forms of Christianity at a rate much greater than at any other time or place in history. These factors signal that the trend toward empowering individuals with both knowledge and wealth will continue to increase for the foreseeable future. As the resulting democracy takes root in a culture, we can be relatively sure that consumer-oriented businesses will be the primary engine of economic growth.

There are many other significant trends that we could also talk about. As the median age of the population grows older with medical breakthroughs, consumer trends change. The invention of air conditioning changed the economy of the South. The "right to work" laws and lower taxes in southern states combined with the invention of air conditioning, quickly made them much more attractive to industries ranging from automotive and aircraft manufacturing to movie studios. There were many visionary people that understood the potential of these trends and placed themselves right where they could benefit the most.

WATCH RULE CHANGES

One major impact on business can be any kind of tax reform. President Reagan's tax reform was badly needed, but so poorly implemented that it not only cost the government billions in revenue, but hundreds of billions in unplanned expenditures. There were inequities, unfairness, burdensome and unnecessary procedures in the previous tax code that needed to be addressed. However, these were the rules on which American business had been built, and by which they had learned to play. When they were changed so quickly, whole industries were caught in unnecessary traps from which most could not escape. The Savings and Loan industry was one of them.

The previous tax code inflated some real estate values because of the tax advantages given to investors. This needed to be corrected but by doing it all at once rather than phasing the changes in over enough time for investors to adjust to them, real estate values on properties such as apartments did not just fall, they collapsed. Because the Savings and Loan industry was holding so much of the paper on such investments, a previously thriving industry was suddenly struggling just to survive. Many Savings and Loans could not make the necessary changes fast enough. The government picked up the tab, which of course went to the taxpayers.

Again, this is not to imply that the changes were not needed. It is also true that the Savings and Loan industry needed stronger regulations to protect investors and depositors from the kind of fraud that was exposed in some places. However, it was not the crooks that brought down the Savings and Loan industry. The implementation of the tax reform was like trying to play a game in which the rules are suddenly changed without warning. What made a winner one day made a big loser the next. Doing the right thing with a little more wisdom and patience would likely have saved the country hundreds of billions of dollars.

As the world continues its trend toward interchange, and inter-dependence, a little change in a government policy in China can have a major impact on a company in Georgia, from shutting it down or suddenly thrusting it into major growth. That is why today's business environment requires watching industry trends, political trends, weather trends, and even spiritual movements. However, gathering the information is just one step. Knowing how to distill and communicate knowledge in its most simple, clear, and effective form, is becoming one of the most valuable skills of all.

Major corporations now hire forecasters whose job is to predict trends. We may not be able to hire forecasters for our own organization, but we can determine the best sources of information we need. We must set aside regular times to study and evaluate the environment in which we are operating, and how it might change. We can then determine just how we might be able to impact conditions with our available resources. Again, as we build our intelligence gathering department or method, the important questions are:

What is happening?

What is not happening?

How can I affect what is happening?

Chapter Eleven

Creating the Future

Now we want to concentrate on how we can use knowledge practically in our sphere of influence. Leadership involves more than just having knowledge and even knowledge about the future. Leadership is the application of knowledge to impact the future. We are not a leader unless someone is following. It is essential for leadership that we also have an ability to communicate our vision of the future in a way that instills enough confidence in others that they are willing to follow us.

Unfortunately, most people do not know who they are, or where they are going. They plod through each day with little vision for the future apart from unrealistic dreams of somehow winning the lottery or stumbling upon the mother lode. Because people were created to live with purpose, to these any plan is inspiring, and motivating. Therefore, basic to effective leadership is first having the ability to formulate a plan, and then having the ability to communicate it.

The communication of a general plan can be done through something as simple as a vision statement or motto. These can be powerful tools for giving purpose and direction to an organization or even a nation. It was Hitler's genius for using simple symbols and one-sentence declarations of a national vision that enabled him to mobilize Germany. The same can be used for good or for evil.

Every organization needs a focused, long-range vision but also shorter ones. For lesser purposes, we might implement a goal for the year, or even a month or week. Such stated purposes and goals will help our organizations stay focused and on track, which will increase efficiency and productivity.

After imparting the general vision, it is the leader's job to devise a workable, step-by-step strategy to accomplish it. We should also establish a way to measure the results of our strategies so that the encouragement of progress is continuous to those we are leading. The confidence this instills will result in the momentum needed for success in any significant venture.

VISION WITH VALUES

All of our goals should be practical and attainable. The more lofty and good that they are, the more that people will tend to be willing to make personal sacrifices to accomplish them. Many have vision but do not have values or at least fail to communicate them along with their vision. Others have values but no vision. Our goal must be to combine vision with values. The power of motivation is not just doubled when we do this but it is multiplied.

The right combination of vision and values is the most powerful force for change the world can ever know. For Alexander the Great, it was to carry the Greek culture, language, and philosophy throughout the world. For the Greeks, who had begun to esteem their seemingly unprecedented refinement of culture and civilization as noble in itself, this was a powerful enough reason for the nation to mobilize and send its sons out to wars of conquest.

For Hitler it was to establish the dominance of the German people. To the Germans who had just lost a war, and were groveling in the worst poverty that existed in Europe, this was a balm for their wounded pride. Any vision was better to them than no vision. This is not to in any way imply that this was right, but as the saying goes, "Deny a man food and he will gobble poison." If the good do not lead and keep the initiative, then the evil will.

It was a similar confusion after the disorienting French Revolution that enabled Napoleon to seize the initiative in France. He simply assuaged French pride and gave them a vision for attaining preeminence in Europe. Any group that is disoriented or without vision can be manipulated and used for evil if the good do not stand up.

No human being can exist long without purpose; neither can a people group. Vision is almost as essential to human existence as oxygen.

Every leader should be aware of the need to define purpose for their organization. Lincoln realized this about the North during the first part of the Civil War. It was not until the Emancipation Proclamation in 1862 that the North felt they had a cause worthy of their mobilization. The struggle then became a noble crusade to free the oppressed. Even the growing anti-war movement was embarrassed to oppose the war, thus the will was acquired to fight until complete victory was attained.

Regardless of the purpose of our organization, the articulation of a clear and noble vision will greatly increase productivity and our chances of success. As stated, few things will keep the energy flowing like having pre-identified smaller goals attained on the way to the bigger one.

Success and failure both breed and multiply. Pride can motivate, but a noble purpose is much better. As the ancient proverb states, "Pride comes before the fall." Pride will always ultimately breed a deadly carelessness. Pride in the form of elitism can motivate and accomplish things for a time, but it has also been repeatedly proven that it will inevitably lead to an ultimate disaster. Our goal must not be just to attain success, but to make it last. Confidence with humility is the platform for true and lasting success.

THE GREAT SKILL

As stated, one common skill of every successful leader is the ability to plan. This is crucial, but with it we must also develop another related skill—the ability to modify, improve, and even change the plan, when necessary.

A good plan is also a motivating factor for any organization. The better the plan, the more confidence it will instill in those we are leading. However, very few situations will ever unfold just like we planned. Therefore, the best plans are those that are resolute enough to instill confidence, while having the flexibility to change with circumstances.

Even though I was in Naval Aviation, like a number of sailors who were temporarily assigned to ground defense forces, I had to go through basic Marine Corps infantry training. I will never forget what one instructor told us. He wore out the need for a battle plan in every engagement, but then finished the class by saying that no battle ever went as planned! In fact, he said the troops that will be victorious will almost always be those that can best deal with confusion and continue to fight.

There is a great truth to this for every venture. A plan will give confidence to the troops, employees, or volunteers, as well as to leaders. However, to win, we will likely have to be wise and flexible enough to know when to throw out some aspects of our plan, or to modify them for the changing situation.

Like generals or business leaders, a good football coach must be good at developing game plans. He may build his whole game plan around his great quarterback, but what if he gets hurt, or is having a bad day? A great coach will know when to change the plan, and usually have contingencies ready. The same should be true of any leader. We must know how to plan, and motivate others to follow the plan, but also know how to lead them in a change of plans. The ability to lead others through the changes without hurting their morale is usually what separates good leaders from great ones.

THE QUICKSAND

For most people their greatest strength is also a root of their greatest weakness. The biggest trap that a gifted planner can fall into is over-planning. Success is the result of action, not just planning. Plans should always be kept simple enough to be easily communicated, easily understood, and easily changed.

Timing is critical in leadership, and timing must take precedence over having a perfect plan before beginning. Many fail because they want to wait until they are perfectly prepared before beginning. We will probably never feel or be perfectly prepared for any initiative.

The decisiveness to move forward even when in an inferior position led to the successes that ultimately caused the Union to win the Civil War under General Grant. Another Union general who many felt was the most gifted was General McClellan. He was probably the best trainer and motivator of troops on either side. However, his tendency to over plan and over prepare cost him victories that would have almost certainly won the war up to three years earlier. At the Battle of Antitem Creek in September of 1862, McClellan's Union Army outnumbered General Lee's Confederate army by more than two to one. McClellan held the best position on the field, and was even given the most extraordinary gift of a copy of Lee's battle plan. He still moved with such hesitancy, and was so indecisive that Lee was able to fight him to a standstill, and escape with his army to fight another day.

IMPROVING IT TO DEATH

Training and planning are necessary, but we must know when to take action. Over planning will lead to "the paralysis of analysis" that will spell defeat. One of the most devastating leadership traps is the tendency to do things too well. If you looked at the first drawings of the greatest artist in the world, you would probably see stick figures. Even the greatest potential artist will never succeed until they are willing to first do something poorly. If we heard the first notes played by a master musician we would almost certainly hear very unpleasant noise. No one starts at the top. The desire to do things too well is possibly the greatest robber of success for the otherwise talented.

We must also avoid the trap of majoring on minors. Perfectionists will sometimes spend most of their time on what produces the least results. In the fad to improve quality in American business, there were many who took it too far, and though quality of many products improved, value went down. How did that happen?

For example, a company would spend a billion dollars to improve quality by 85 percent. They would then have to double that amount to get another 5 percent improvement. They would then have to quadruple that amount to get another 1 percent. There is a point where further improvement is not worth what we have to pay for it. In this case our goal should probably be an 85 percent improvement. Perfection is not a realistic goal on this earth but quality with value will be successful.

It was also interesting to watch American business jump on the re-engineering fad. It is good to continually improve our process, but there can be a delusion in thinking that getting the process right is the answer to all of our problems. This only enabled many companies to make the wrong products better.

Another trap can be to make too much of an effort to learn from our mistakes. This has been called "making yesterday perfect." It is always good to learn from the past, and mistakes will be one of our greatest teachers, but we must not focus on this at the expense of the present or future. Learn as much as you can and then start moving.

Many great leaders are defeated because they try to accomplish too much or fight battles on too many fronts. We must as much as we are able choose our own battles and battlefields. A basic military strategy was once stated as "He who gets there first with the most wins." To do this we must be able to concentrate our forces or resources. Do not allow yourself to be spread too thin by trying to accomplish too much.

Another trap is to become overly focused on money. This is not to say that we do not need some focus on money, but the key word here is *overly*. Even though this is the economic age, money is often the least important resource for any organization. If you do what you are called to do with excellence, resolve, and wisdom, money will come to you. If you are overly focused on money you will tend to wait until you have enough of it to start but you will probably never feel that you have enough. Be wise in gathering your resources but do not be overly focused on this one issue and it will come to you much faster.

CHAPTER TWELVE

CULTIVATING VISION

Cultivating vision is a practical way that we can increasingly open our eyes to see beyond the things that are, and see the way they could be. Vision that sees beyond the present is the foundation of leadership. In this chapter we will review and elaborate on a few of the basic things that will help to open our eyes, and enable us to lead in a way that will turn what we see into a reality.

Effective leaders will accomplish their own goals; great leaders dictate the course of history. As we have discussed, you are not a leader unless someone will follow you. Only a fool will follow someone who does not know where they are going. The more clear and noble the vision, the better the people will be who you attract.

Great leaders have the ability to make other leaders into followers. The quality of those who follow you will directly reflect the quality of your accomplishment. To make other leaders into followers requires a greater depth of character, commitment, and vision. The more intelligent and noble your goals, the more intelligent and noble your followers will be.

Martin Luther King, Jr. was a great leader. He shared his dream with such conviction that it became the dream of millions of others. I heard it said by one of his associates that during the meetings with other civil rights leaders he would sit patiently, intently listening to everything that was said. He was genuinely concerned with what others believed, and considered it important to understand. Then he would inevitably be asked to share his thoughts. Whenever he spoke in these meetings his words came with such profound understanding, clarity of purpose, and confidence in his direction that there was little left to be said when he finished.

Great leaders are usually more inclined to listen than to speak. Therefore, when they do speak, it is with greater substance. Great leaders will also be great communicators. Some seem to come by this more naturally than others, but it is a talent that can be developed. Practice articulating your thoughts as concisely as possible. As the biblical proverb states, "Like apples of gold in settings of silver is a word spoken in right circumstances." Such words fit and compliment each other.

ENNOBLE YOUR LEADERSHIP

Great leaders have seldom taken the mantle of leadership for its own sake. True leadership is born out of vision and strategy that is established firmly on the bedrock of conviction and purpose. Leadership is a means and not the end in itself. By keeping this in mind we can ennoble our specific, material goals. Few will be inspired if your goal is to be the biggest company in a certain field (specific goal), but many might become inspired if your goal for doing this is to better the economic conditions of your community, help send the children of your faithful, long-term employees to college, to build your own retirement resort, etc.

The ability to be a great visionary is to a degree a spiritual gift that some seem to just be born with. However, many who seem to naturally have this gift, lack other characteristics such as resolve, steadfastness, etc., to make their visions a reality. Such are dreamers who may talk a lot but seldom do much. There are many others who have all the characteristics to take a vision and make it a reality but have difficulty formulating the vision. This ability to see the future differently can be cultivated by those who desire it enough to apply themselves.

By definition, a vision is a concept that is not yet real. The first step in formulating a vision is to simply start thinking about what could be rather than what presently exists. This does take a certain amount of optimism; the critical and skeptical will seldom have visions or dreams.

To be optimistic is no small feat—recent studies revealed that almost 70 percent of the average person's thoughts are negative (thinking something bad about someone or something, or expecting something bad to happen.) The shocking fact of this study was that these were Americans who tend to be the most optimistic people in the world! Why do we allow ourselves to live in such mental misery? Such people live lives that are mostly bitter, and fall well below their potential. Only those who believe that they can succeed will be encouraged enough to put forth the effort that it takes to succeed.

The single most important step that most of us can take to start becoming a visionary, and then turning our visions into successes, is to start thinking the very best about everything and everyone. Even if we are sometimes wrong by doing this, it is much better to err on the side of believing in others, not to mention the fact that our lives will become infinitely more enjoyable! This will open us up to disappointments, but there are things much worse than occasionally being disappointed—we can fail to do what we otherwise could have accomplished.

Every event that takes place in our lives will either make us bitter or better, but the choice is ours. There will always be some people and situations that fail or disappoint us, but it is a well-established fact that people perform much better with positive motivation than negative threats. If we want to get the most and the best out of our people we must therefore maintain a positive attitude about them. This does not mean that we abandon wisdom, or overlook warnings. We must always keep in mind that the accomplishment of any significant vision will take significant people, and significant people will almost always need to be led in a positive way.

VISION BEGINS WHERE WE ARE

You can start practicing vision right where you are. Start by looking at your job and listing all of the positive things about it. Then begin a list of things that could make it better. Next, determine that you are going to accomplish these and make it the very best job that it can be.

Then start practicing this in every area of your life. If your marriage is not going well, determine that you are going to make it better. If you would bring your wife flowers occasionally, she may desire to lose weight. If you do nice things for your husband, he may stop complaining about the petty things you do that bother him. What is your vision for your marriage or your family? What can you do to help get it there?

Take this gift of seeing to new levels by confronting negative things or people in your life with the determination to make them better. If you really want to take this to a higher level, choose to see positive things about the most negative thing or person in your life. What can you do to make it better? Who is your worst enemy? What could you do to turn them into a friend? You may not be able to do this quickly, but what could you do to begin to make that person feel more positive toward you?

The measure of who you were in this life will be remembered mostly by those things that you were able to make better than they were. Practice this in every area of your life. Count your successes and measure your progress. You'll find that each success will lead to other bigger ones. If you learn what it takes to turn your marriage around, you may be able to then turn a company around, or a neighborhood. If you do this, your neighbors may then want you to run for mayor to turn your city around.

Build your life on successes and advancement and you will grow in the ability to improve the conditions of everything and everyone in your life. It will become natural to see that everything and everyone can be better, which is the essence of vision.

RECORD THE VISION

Take a few minutes to write down the goals that came to your mind as you read the above. To help, you might want to answer the following questions.

> *General Life Goal:* What is the most important goal that you want to accomplish in your life? (Possible answers might be to write a book, build a business, get elected to a public office, become a church leader, etc.)

> *Family Goal:* What is the most important goal for your family? (Consider each member separately. You might ask them their goals and make yours seeing them all accomplished).

> *Financial Goal:* What is your personal financial goal? (It might be anything from owning your home and being out of debt by a certain age, to attaining a certain net worth, etc.)

Pleasure Goal: What is your greatest goal for recreation or pleasure? (This could include such things as owning a vacation home, a boat, becoming a private pilot, etc.)

It would be helpful for you to write each goal in a journal so that you can review each one periodically to measure your progress. This leads us to the foundational talent of all successful leaders.

DEVELOPING A PLAN

As stated, developing a plan is the main characteristic that separates the *achievers* from the dreamers. Even if we have the most noble and appropriate goals, our chances of accomplishing them are remote without proper planning.

More than genius, it was probably Napoleon's commitment to planning that made him so much more successful than the rival generals he defeated. He studied incessantly, pouring over the maps of potential battlefields, intelligence reports of the disposition and strength of the enemy, even the character and history of opposing generals.

Like most enterprises, battles are seldom executed as planned. Napoleon was such a tireless planner that he fought the battle many times in his mind before the real one took place. This helped prepare him for meeting each contingency. He would have his revised plan being implemented while his adversaries were just getting out their maps to start thinking about what they should do next. Because of his planning, he was almost always able to stay one step ahead of his opponents, keeping them on the defensive and taking advantage of opportunities that were not available to those less prepared. Good planning disciplines can do the same for us.

Planning is both an art and a discipline. Even the greatest artist must develop his skills; so must the leader develop his ability to plan. Effective planning requires the ability to assimilate and organize facts concerning the realities being dealt with. Then we must be able to observe the facts in a way that will produce insights leading to advantage and success. Let's briefly break down this process into its three basic parts:

1. *State the goal(s).* This was done in our previous exercise. Planning requires an ability to visualize the future and then to make a road map for navigating it. We will never know where to make the road if we do not know where we want to go.

2. *Getting and organizing the necessary facts.* The ability to do research is a significant skill within itself. We must determine first where we can get the best and most relevant facts to help us. How do we sift through all of the information available to us to get just what we need? This is where many leaders get bogged down—being concept oriented rather than detail oriented. This is the point where their leadership potential is often lost.

3. *Making the plan.* As stated previously, the first step in making a good plan is the realization that the plan can be changed. Therefore, do not worry about having to make a perfect plan because adjustments can be made as you go.

Take the goals that you have already listed and write out a plan for each one. Write questions that come to your mind such as: What is the first step I need to take? What will the subsequent steps be? What may present obstacles to accomplishing the goal? What can present opportunities for accomplishing it? What resources are needed? What resources are available? Who has accomplished this goal before and how did they do it? It might be good to layout one year, five year plans, etc.

After your plan is finished, you may want to play the deadly enemy game. If you were the enemy of your plan, what would you do to stop it? This will help you to see potential weaknesses or serious problems that are not apparent.

This chapter was a review and an attempt to sink our roots a little deeper into what we have already covered for the sake of retention. The goal for this book is not just to teach leadership principles, but also to inspire better leaders. That will only happen if we retain and implement what is learned. Leaders do not just know what to do—they do it.

CHAPTER THIRTEEN

CHARACTER, WILL, AND WISDOM

Regardless of their brilliance, history testifies that even the most outstanding leaders will ultimately fail unless their lives have the underpinnings of honor, morality, and character. In this part we will examine in more depth the characteristics that constitute this essential foundation for success in leadership. The first is:

THE WILL

In the last chapter we covered the essential need for leaders to have vision and the ability to formulate a workable plan. Many have had these abilities and still failed because they did not have the resolve, courage, and endurance to press on to completion of the goal.

"Knowledge is power" according to a biblical proverb. Knowledge is essential for accomplishing every endeavor, so we will do well to seek knowledge. However, without adding to our knowledge, wisdom, and courage, we will probably accomplish very little, regardless of how vast our knowledge is. Wisdom is the *ability* to apply knowledge correctly. Courage is the *will* to apply it. Without wisdom and courage, increased knowledge will only inflict us with "the paralysis of analysis." Planning and preparation must lead to action—the implementation of our plans.

As stated, it is unlikely that we will ever feel, or be totally prepared and confident when it is time to begin. It will, therefore, take great courage to make the first step. Often circumstances come upon us suddenly, requiring action when we feel totally unprepared. In these situations it seems that once we begin to take action to the best of our ability, confidence and wisdom will come. A leader must be action-oriented and not solely a whiz at theory and planning. The ability to plan is essential for true success but it must be united with the will to move into action.

A leader, like the captain of a ship, needs to know where he's going and how to get there *before* he leaves port. He must also be able to make adjustments in his plans during the journey. Changes will be necessary after the storms, mechanical failures, and other surprises have occurred. It is important to have the resolution to stay on course when possible, but it is just as important to know when to adjust the course, or to get back on it when a deviation has been required. Had that wisdom been with Captain Smith of the Titanic, it is likely that his ship would never have sunk. Resolve to hold the course is important, but it can be deadly when it is not balanced with wisdom.

KEEP YOUR PRIORITIES

Many have their leadership abilities sapped by majoring on minors. A popular saying in business today is "count the pennies and the dollars will take care of themselves." This is probably true because if the leader of an organization is taking time to count the pennies, there probably will not be any dollars to worry about! Get someone else to count the pennies! The leader must major on the majors.

If we do not take control of our own time, that which represents 10 percent or less of our enterprise will demand 90 percent of our attention. In many cases this is the cause of burnout for the leader and substantial losses for the enterprise. If we're in leadership we must learn to delegate the details, and give our attention to leading and planning. This is a challenge for leaders who are doers by nature and are inclined to become too involved—but it must be done if we are to fulfill our potential.

Learning to prioritize your duties can actually multiply your productivity. A simple classification system can be helpful. Keep a current list of your "Things To Do." If under your classification system number 1 is the highest priority, do not work on the 2's until the 1's are finished, and so forth down the line. A few more pennies may fall through the cracks but you'll be amazed at how many more dollars come in!

If we are going to keep our priorities in their proper order, we must be delivered from the curse of self-centeredness. Few empires, civilizations, or enterprises have been overthrown by enemies without— they have almost all perished from the cancer of self-centeredness, which is often the result of their prosperity. Cancer is a cell that consumes for its own purposes without regard to the rest of the body. In a sense, cancer is the personification of self-centeredness.

To prevent this we must establish predetermined personal morals and values that will not be compromised, even for the sake of the success of our enterprise. What are they? Is lying, and therefore becoming a liar worth the success we are after? Is our success worth the hurt that a certain course will inflict upon others? To win World War II the answers to these questions may have been "yes." Using deception to foil the enemy was crucial to the success of many operations. At times a course had to be chosen that would inflict casualties on civilians, but had with it the possibility of ending the war more quickly and thereby saving others. Leadership sometimes requires very difficult choices.

In many areas, Western civilization has risen to the highest standards of honor, justice, morality, and the esteem for life. It is apparent that these qualities are the foundation of western progress. Now those foundations are being tested. The issue of abortion is one of the tests. Some feel that it will ultimately be as divisive as slavery was in the last century, or that it even has the potential to surpass it. Some view abortion as an issue of freedom, and some as the value we will give to life, and the ultimate freedom—the freedom to live at all.

In nature, preservation of life is the most basic and powerful motivation. Because of this, excepting only a few of the most base forms of species, *family* is a primary drive of life. There are few creatures in existence that will not quickly and instinctively sacrifice their own lives to protect their young. It therefore seems to have been no accident that the very first test of King Solomon's wisdom was concerning the issue of a mother's sanctity for life. The very first test of wisdom for any government is its commitment to the sanctity of life. However, some feel that a woman's freedom and ability to live her life as she chooses supersedes her unborn child's right to live at all.

These are basic issues. We now are confronted with the very real possibility of cloning, defining our values, and definitions of life that may have huge and terrible consequences, which we will face as a civilization. When Germany succumbed to the ideas of a master race, they were soon destroying all who were physically or mentally inferior to their definition of what the German people were to be. Some of the great souls in history would not have passed the test to deserve life in Nazi Germany, as tens of thousands of children disappeared. This great nation went from being one of the most civilized and noble to stark barbarity in just a few years.

It is unnatural for a mother to destroy her child, born or unborn, and it reveals a fundamental departure from civilization to embrace a barbarism in its most base and inhuman form. The resolution of the abortion issue gives us the opportunity to provide the world leadership in finding even higher standards of morality, justice, and the esteem for life. The failure to resolve it with courage and honor, not just with law, will certainly leave a major crack in our foundation of honor and morality, and can eventually lead to an ultimate form of tyranny.

Because something is legal does not make it right. There are fundamental laws that prevail in nature which reveal a great deal more wisdom than politicians often display. True morality does not have much to do with mere legal compliance; true morality is doing what is right regardless of what we are able to get away with. A civilization that is not based on law will be open to despotism and tyranny. But a civilization that cannot rise above the law to live by what is not just legal but also moral, has lost its humanity and its potential for true greatness. Lawlessness always results in tyranny. The inability to rise above law will also result in tyranny. The preservation of life is fundamental to both nature and morality.

Even so, can we cast stones at the mother who aborts her child if we ourselves are sacrificing our living children at the altars of the petty gods of selfish ambition and personal success? Could even the greatest success of our enterprises be interpreted as anything but a terrible human failure if we lose our own children in the process? Who can count the "successful" businessmen, sportsmen, coaches and even church leaders, who have accomplished their goals only to say that they would trade everything just to have their families back again. The first condition that God identified as not good was for man to be alone. Loneliness is not good, and that is exactly where we will end up if we do not give our families the priority they deserve.

This book is not intended to be a family-counseling manual. However, if you have a family, they will almost certainly either be a great source of motivation or a great burden which detracts from your venture. How you value your family will almost certainly be up to you. If your love for your family is more than your enterprise, then everything else is subsequently increased. A decline in productivity usually parallels the devotion to selfishness. We were created to need others, and the motivation of doing things for others is one of the highest motivations. Family is primordial. History testifies that the quickest way to destroy a civilization is to destroy the moral fabric which is rooted in the esteem for family. All other standards of meaning and morality are easily overthrown if the basic drive of life, the family, is diluted.

After our immediate family, the next on our priority list should be people. Do we see our venture as a "thing" or as the people who comprise it? People are more important than things. As your venture is personalized, some of the more powerful motivations for success will energize your people. As much as possible, a primary goal of the leader should be to get his people to see themselves as a family. Such an identity will be your best chance to stir them to self-sacrifice in place of the self-centeredness that always works against the basic vision and purpose of your venture.

STEADFASTNESS

Steadfastness was originally a navy term used for the ability to stay on course. Also added to this was the ability to keep returning to the course after a deviation was necessary until the goal is accomplished. To achieve this the goal must have more power in your life than the multitude of external pressures which will try to deter you from the course. The ability to do this will depend mostly upon how well you have prepared for the journey to accomplishment, with its conflicts and storms.

As an aircraft pilot, several times I have been caught in storms so rough I could not read my charts. I would have been in serious trouble had I not taken the time to *prepare* for the flight. During those storms I was thankful I had not taken any shortcuts in my training, and that I was conscientious enough to study my flight path prior to take-off.

In preparation for every flight, I would memorize the important frequencies and headings, along with an alternate airport with good weather that I could reach with my available fuel. I regularly reviewed emergency procedures for possible engine failure, which instruments I would lose if my vacuum, electrical, or other systems failed, and how I could compensate for their loss, etc. On the majority of my flights this may have all seemed like a waste of time, but there were a few occasions when I knew that all my effort in planning and training had been worth it. I have had several engine failures, experienced lightning strikes, electrical fires, and have been blown far off course by storms. In most of these incidents my pulse hardly even quickened because I was *prepared* and knew what to do. A lack of preparedness can result in panic that is potentially more deadly than the emergency. Every enterprise will have emergencies. Our preparation during times of relative calm will have much to do with our performance during the crisis.

Peace of mind is one of the most valuable assets of a leader. Worry clouds our judgment and saps much more energy than actual physical exertion. Stress is also the worst enemy of clear thinking and planning. Besides preparation for the course, there are other factors that will help us to keep our peace of mind.

General Robert E. Lee and Stonewall Jackson were pious men who had a genuine belief that there was One higher than they who ordered the affairs of men. This enabled them to maintain a peace of mind even during the times of greatest conflict, confusion, and pressure. Some historians have suggested that it was the principal advantage that these great generals had over their opponents. Peace of mind is certainly one of the best human possessions and advantages that we can have in life, and it should be a goal in itself. Worry will never cause what we want to happen, or keep what we do not want from happening—it is a trivial, useless exercise that is unworthy of the true leader.

ENDURANCE

Endurance is the ability to stay with the task all the way to *completion*, which is similar to steadfastness. This is a serious problem with those who have strong leadership ability because leaders typically find it much more stimulating to start a task than to finish it. As a result they often have numerous unfinished projects lying dormant while they pick up the pursuit of the next interesting venture.

The ability to finish the job is every bit as important as being able to get all of the resources and energy going to start it. This takes *discipline*.

The failure to complete a job is usually a telltale sign that we are running on emotional energy rather than true, focused vision. This is the reason some of the world's best salesmen remain poor; they can get an Eskimo excited about buying snow, but somehow they never get his signature on the bottom line. These salesmen get a sense of accomplishment out of persuading their prospects to believe them—not in getting their business. We have not succeeded *until* the job is completed!

INTEGRITY

Integrity is more than just being honest; it is doing what is *right*. It is the freedom from corrupting influence or practice, while practicing what you preach. It is doing what your conscience tells you to do even if it leaves you as a committee of one. It is the courage to stand by your convictions. It is always reaching for higher moral standards than may be customary in the group, for the true leader is always reaching for higher standards. It is also the courage and honesty to admit mistakes and failures, and to accept the blame for them.

Even the greatest leaders make mistakes. The better the leader you are, the more costly and visible your mistakes will be. Recovering from mistakes is an important test of true leadership ability. Complete recovery will not take place without accepting such mistakes and taking responsibility for them. The greatest leaders learn to turn their failures into opportunities for achievement and victory. In many cases failures will turn into the best opportunities for victory. Wellington, Napoleon, and Lee accomplished some of their greatest victories because of their ability to turn their enemy's achievements into a trap for defeating them. The Japanese used defeat in war as a springboard for economic victory in peacetime. Vision and leadership can turn the worst catastrophe into opportunity.

To his credit, General Lee never blamed anyone but himself for the defeat at Gettysburg. His subordinates failed him a number of times in that battle. The compounded effect of those failures led him to make the desperate decision that led to defeat. But Lee never mentioned any of his subordinate's failures. After the war when one of these generals publicly and bitterly blamed Lee for the defeat, Lee agreed with him. This humility endeared him to the entire world, and he actually became the most respected man in the nation after the war—even among the Northerners. His humility soon caused even his worst critics to acknowledge him as one of the great men of their times. When he passed away, the entire nation mourned the son they all wanted to claim as their own.

Historians have declared that Lee's leadership after his defeat was probably greater than that which he displayed in war. Almost all agree that his leadership in helping to bring reconciliation between the North and South was more important for the restoration of the nation than any other single factor. Lee set a standard of personal integrity, reconciliation, and forgiveness. His leadership after the war almost certainly prevented years of guerrilla warfare and further destruction in a nation that desperately needed healing.

A great leader must possess the confidence and security to accept the truth about himself and the consequences of his actions. The greatest leaders are those who can best deal with failure—because all will fail at one time or another. Those who boast that they have never failed have never really played the game. But failure truly can be a great opportunity for future success, if we learn the lessons it teaches instead of just making excuses. As the saying goes, "He who is good at making excuses is seldom good at anything else." The greatest victories are those that overcome previous defeats.

Those who follow or work for you deserve to know the facts. People usually see far more than the average leader gives them credit for. When leaders are not straightforward about problems and mistakes they can be viewed as dishonest, or unable to see reality, ultimately resulting in a deterioration of morale and commitment. Motivation and loyalty that has depth and staying power is founded upon truth, not hype.

Honesty is also an essential requirement for peace of mind. We'll never have peace if we're worried about someone finding us out. Whatever we may gain by cheating or lying is not worth the price we pay when we are forty years old with an eighty year-old heart. Honesty brings respect and inspires those who may serve under us more than almost anything else we can do. The self-respect we gain from being honest will pay higher dividends in the long run than anything we might gain through deception.

COURAGE

Courage is the quality of mind and heart that makes us resist the temptation to stop or retreat in the face of opposition, danger, or hardship. This implies the summoning of all our powers to reach the goal. Courage is the firmness of spirit and moral backbone that, while appreciating and properly measuring the risks involved, makes us press on until success is accomplished.

Obstacles and roadblocks will precede the attainment of almost any worthy goal. How we deal with these problems will determine our success or failure. There are four basic ways that people deal with problems; two of these ways lead to certain failure, one of them will make success more difficult but may still leave the potential for it. Only one of these ways of dealing with problems is *likely* to lead to success. Let us consider them each separately.

1. The first way we can respond to an obstacle is to let it turn us back. This course leads to failure and reveals the lack of courage, resolve, and leadership required for success in any enterprise.

2. The second way is to let the obstacle stop us. We may not retreat or turn back, but we no longer advance either. Even if we hold on to our dream or goal, and allow obstacles to stop us, we will be perpetually defeated and frustrated.

3. The third way to deal with an obstacle is to let it change our course. There are some obstacles we meet which require a change in our plans that would make this option the best one. Just changing our course may still allow us to go on to ultimate success, *but if we are prone to letting obstacles change our course too easily the chances of our success will greatly decrease.*

It takes real wisdom to know when to change our plan. Sometimes we must let wisdom overrule courage and resolve if we are going to succeed. It may have required more courage and resolve for Hitler to insist on taking Stalingrad, but it was also unwise and it led to his ultimate defeat, not just at Stalingrad, but also for the entire war. To conquer Stalingrad was one of Hitler's goals, but it was not essential for accomplishing his overall goal of conquering Russia. If he had just gone around that city he probably could have accomplished his ultimate goal. His insistence on taking that one fortress resulted in the wasting of an entire army, needlessly destroyed in that one battle. Resolve and courage are essential, but they must be controlled by intelligence.

4. The fourth way to deal with an obstacle is to *overcome* it by driving it out of your way instead of allowing it to drive you off of your course. This is usually the best way to deal with an obstacle and should be our first approach.

Courage is essential to leadership but it must be tempered with vision and strategy, always keeping our ultimate goal in the forefront so that we are not defeated by our secondary successes. George

Washington is a good study in how to balance courage with the keeping of our vision on the ultimate goal. Many times ambitious men would rise to seek his position as Commander-in-Chief of the Continental Army. Often he was tempted to defend himself and attack the integrity of those lesser men. He resisted that temptation knowing such pettiness could undo the unity of the thirteen states, and result in their defeat by the British. It took more courage for Washington to stay above the political infighting than it did to get elected.

LOYALTY

Loyalty is faithfulness to principles, the plan, and people. A social chameleon that will change to conform to each new environment or group is void of the basic characteristics that make a true leader. True leaders are not so easily changed but instead have the strength of character to change their environments or the mindset of the crowd.

If we are to expect others to be loyal to us, we must set the example. If we possess loyalty we will not stoop to gossip or belittle others in leadership or subordinates. The true leader does not rise by making others look smaller. Great leaders will always set the highest standards, not follow what others may or may not be doing.

INITIATIVE

Obviously a leader has to be one who seeks and accepts respon- sibility. Half of the victory is often found in just starting the battle. The ones who take initiative will usually be able to keep it, giving them a substantial advantage.

It has been said that there are basically three kinds of people in the world: those who watch what is happening, those who talk about making things happen, *and those who actually do it.* The sad thing is that most of those in the first two categories have everything required to be a *doer* except one thing—initiative. Many of the greatest athletes never play in a real game because they never took the first step to try out for the team. If those who spend their lives dreaming about being great musicians would spend as much time practicing as they do dreaming, others would be dreaming about being them! Few of those who always talk about doing great things ever do anything at all, much less anything great. Every journey begins with just one step; if you do not know how to take it, you are not going to go anywhere.

CHAPTER FOURTEEN

COURAGE THAT CHANGED THE WORLD

This is a brief, inspirational story about the exploits of the Knights of St. John during the Middle Ages. It includes some of the greatest historic examples of what can be accomplished by those who live by the highest principles of leadership. Against odds, which some historians estimated to be more than one hundred to one, these brave knights took their stand against the most powerful armies of the age and prevailed. Their history is worthy of recounting as one of the greatest examples of leadership the world has produced.

During the time when Christian Europe succumbed to increasing division and internal conflict, the Islamic Ottoman Empire was unifying the Moslem world. Having finally driven the Crusaders from Palestine, Islam turned its attention to the conquest of Europe. Because of the conflicts within Europe, there was no one who could raise a Christian army to stand against the hoards from the East. To the Turks, Europe now appeared as an open treasure chest.

In 1309, the Knights of the Order of St. John conquered the island of Rhodes. This island was situated precariously almost within sight of the heart of the Ottoman Empire, but the knights saw it as convenience. The Order quickly began building fortifications, and Rhodean seaman, who for centuries had been the best in the world, taught their skills to the knights. The Order built ships and began to raid Moslem shipping. This quickly made them odious to the Ottomans, but the knights only increased the boldness of their raids. However, the Order was so efficient in their sea war that the Ottomans were discouraged from even trying to become a great sea power.

As the Order became a serious threat to the supply lines of the Islamic armies massing to conquer Western Europe, it was determined that something had to be done. Finally, Mehmet became Sultan, and soon became one of the most distinguished leaders in history. He was a brilliant man who was fluent in a half dozen languages, and possessed extensive knowledge of literature and science. Mehmet quickly raised the cultural and military excellence of his people to a level which surpassed the great nations of Europe. Becoming increasingly irritated with the knights, he determined that he would send a force to eradicate the nuisance.

Even though the monarchs of Europe were glad that the knights were at least distracting the Turks, they scorned them as "archaic relics from the past." When the Order requested supplies and reinforcements to stand against the impending invasion of the Moslem army, all of Europe refused to help them. They considered the little Order to be doomed and any help given to them would therefore be a waste. Even so, the knights determined not to retreat, vowing to accept death rather than to yield a single acre of ground to the enemies of the cross.

THE FIRST BATTLE OF RHODES

The theology of Jihad was then popular in Islam. Jihad is a Holy War to conquer the world by force for Allah. War was therefore glorified, and death in Jihad guaranteed one their place in heaven regardless of previous sins. When the religious leaders proclaimed a conflict to be a Jihad the doors of heaven were opened to anyone who gave their life for the cause. Multitudes saw this as their opportunity to gain heaven in spite of their previous debauchery, so they actually hoped to die in battle. This made the warriors of Islam some of the most deadly and feared that the world had ever seen.

Mehmet was also a conqueror at heart who fashioned himself after Alexander the Great. He marched on the great city of Constantinople and conquered it. He then set his sights on the rest of Europe. But before he could take the rest of Europe, he had to do something about the annoying knights at Rhodes who continued to plunder his shipping and supply lines.

In 1480, Mehmet sent his most able generals with an army of 70,000 men to subdue the 600 knights and 1,500 to 2,000 militia at

Rhodes. Even though the knights were so few, they had proven so capable in previous conflicts that Mehmet wanted to take no chances. It appeared to all that the siege of Rhodes would be brief and decisive.

After landing his army, Mehmet's siege cannons began to batter the walls the Order had spent over a century building. Numerous other cannons hurled projectiles over the walls into the city. The Grand Master of the Order was a Frenchman named d'Aubusson. He was a remarkable leader of men who had with great foresight prepared his knights for the siege he knew would one day come. He had even built shelters for the townspeople so that they could escape the bombardment. Knowing that they could expect little or no help from Europe, d'Aubusson nevertheless had determined that they would stand as long as one knight could draw a bow or wield a sword.

In early June, after days of bombardment, the first wave of assault troops attacked the Tower of St. Nicholas, an outlying fortification of the city. The Moslems were shocked by the stiff resistance they met and were repulsed with many casualties. They immediately began another general bombardment that would hurl over a thousand cannon balls a day at the city for several weeks. The walls began to collapse while the Turks snaked closer and closer with their trenches. At night, fires burned everywhere from the grenades and incendiaries. Those who were present declared that a scene out of hell itself could be no worse. Still the knights held their ground.

On June 18, the Turks launched a second human wave assault led by the fearsome Janissaries, renowned as the greatest fighters in the world. Each Janissary had been chosen from age seven because of their physical potential and trained their entire lives for combat. They had been forbidden to marry or engage in any kind of family affections in order to focus all of their emotions and energy on battle. The assault began under the cover of darkness because they expected to find the knights sleeping, but they were wrong. Swords, arrows, and gunfire filled the night. As the sun rose, it revealed legions of Janissary bodies filling the moats around the tower of St. Nicholas, and the knights still standing on the battered walls.

The disbelieving Turkish generals had never experienced such a military setback. They turned to subterfuge to pry the knights from their fortress city. They planted agents in the city by having them pretend to be defectors to the Christians (many of the Sultan's troops were captives from Christian nations). These spies were soon able to create serious tactical problems for the knights, who were being pressed from within and without. Each day presented a new crisis that threatened their very existence. The fortifications were crumbling everywhere, even at the most strategic points. Still they held on. Then the Turks began massing for a final great assault that both sides fully expected to be the end.

The great attack began on July 27. The knights and the remaining militia took their positions on what was left of the walls. The Sultan sent his Bashi-Bazouk troops first. These were mercenaries who were considered expendable, and wave after wave were cut down by the defenders. Their bodies soon filled the ditches and streams, making human bridges that led up to the walls, which had in fact been the strategy of the Turkish generals. Then the tired and wounded defenders watched as great waves of the fearsome Janissaries arose and advanced, even more resolute now because of their previous humiliation.

The Turks quickly overwhelmed the strategic Tower of St. Nicholas, which had taken the brunt of the main assault for nearly two months. As promised, the knights contested every acre of ground, for which the Turks paid dearly. With an arrow in his thigh, d'Aubusson led a dozen knights and three standard bearers up a ladder and onto the wall. There d'Aubusson received four more wounds before a Janissary of gigantic size hurled a spear right through his breastplate, puncturing his lung. He was dragged out of the fray just as the enemy made a breach in the defenses and began to pour into the city. It appeared certain that the end of the Knights of St. John had finally come.

In hand to hand combat, over burning rubble, through choking smoke and fire, in possibly the worst hell that men could create for themselves on the earth, the Turks continued to throw themselves against the remaining knights. Even so, the tenacity of those knights, and their ability to inflict casualties, astonished, and soon disheartened the Turks. Even the resolve of the Janissaries was shaken as row after row of men continued to be cut down by the defenders. Still the battle raged on.

Then, above the smoke and turmoil of this terrible inferno, on the one remaining parapet, d'Aubusson's standards suddenly appeared. They were held by three bearers in shining armor who appeared almost as gods from the hell below. The effect on the Moslems was electrifying as a wave of fear swept through the army. The remaining Bashi began to flee in such terror that it overcame the Janissaries. Then the entire

Moslem army began to melt away in confusion, retreating at the very moment when total victory was easily within their grasp.

As the Moslems fled, Rhodian sharpshooters on the walls poured a deadly fire into them. The remaining knights amazingly found enough strength to counterattack, chasing the Sultan's troops all the way to their base camp. Within ten days the shattered army that had been the pride of the Ottoman Empire fled the island. To the astonishment of the entire world the Order of St. John had not only survived—they had prevailed. All of Europe celebrated. All of Islam was enraged.

ISLAM IN CHECK

That decimation of the great army of the seemingly unconquerable Mehmet, by such a small force, was viewed as a military miracle of biblical proportions. The Order that had been viewed by Europe as "an archaic relic of the past," was elevated to a new prominence, and was now viewed as the savior of the continent. But the knights wasted little time celebrating; they immediately began to rebuild their fortifications, expecting an even greater assault to now come. They were right.

The Ottomans could not advance any further into Europe with the knights holding Rhodes and threatening their lines of supply. The knights knew they were now more odious than ever to the Sultan, and they were also too weakened to endure another assault. They prayed for a reprieve from heaven and received it. Mehmet raised another, even larger army for a second attack on Rhodes, which he intended to personally lead, but on his way south, he became sick and died. The knights considered this a miracle. The knights were given a little more time to heal their wounds and repair the walls before the next onslaught. Fittingly, even d'Aubusson survived his wounds.

As the Order continued preparations for the next battle with their characteristic resolve, it was as if they knew the world's destiny had been cast upon their shoulders. Now money and munitions poured into the tiny island from Europe, and almost all of it was devoted to the reconstruction of the walls and towers. The army of the Crescent would not return to Rhodes for forty years, but it would take that long for the Order to prepare for what was coming.

In 1503, d'Aubusson died, but his vision and leadership insured that the fortress would grow even stronger than it had been before the first siege. These efforts were not wasted—an even greater test was coming. Meanwhile, Europe was also being given desperately needed time to regroup.

SULEIMAN ASCENDS

In 1520 "Suleiman the Magnificent" ascended to the throne of the Ottoman Empire. Like Mehmet, he was a man of culture and learning, as well as a brilliant general. Under his leadership the empire would rise to its greatest heights, and its power was without rival in the world.

One year later, Phillippe Villiers de L'Isle Adam became the Grand Master of the Order of St. John. L'Isle Adam was likewise an educated aristocrat, as well as an experienced seaman and a devout Christian. He would also prove to be a great leader. The main players for another one of history's most strategic conflicts were now in place.

In 1521, the Sultan sent the newly elected Grand Master "A Letter of Victory," in which he boasted of his recent victories and asked that the Grand Master "rejoice with me over my triumphs." L'Isle Adam was more direct than diplomatic; he replied that he fully understood the meaning of the letter—that Suleiman intended to make Rhodes his next conquest.

The Sultan's next letter demanded that Rhodes be surrendered to him at once. The Sultan's timing was typically brilliant. Henry VIII of England was in the process of seizing the Order's properties in Britain. France and Spain were at war, and Italy was already devastated. Again, the Order could expect no help or reinforcements. A few hundred gallant knights would again have to stand alone against the most powerful army on earth.

THE SECOND BATTLE OF RHODES

By June 1522, Suleiman was ready for his assault on Rhodes. Historians estimate that the Sultan assembled up to 700 ships and 200,000 men for the attack. Even allowing for natural exaggeration, this was an overwhelming force to come against 500 knights and an estimated 1,500 militia. On July 28, the Sultan himself landed on Rhodes with a grand salute, and the battle began.

The Turks brought up their huge siege guns, capable of hurling balls nine feet in circumference. These were added to a multitude of other cannons and mortars assembled for the bombardment. Throughout the month of August they poured thousands of cannon balls into the city and its fortified positions each day. The knights answered with their own artillery, much smaller, but devastatingly accurate on the relatively unprotected Turks.

By the end of August, a number of breeches began to appear in the fortress walls. In early September, the first infantry assault came. Typically, the knights contested every point, but the overwhelming numbers pushed back the defenders until the Turks were able to plant their standards on the wall itself. Never had the knights lost that much ground in the first attack. They counter attacked with the Grand Master himself entering the fray. After a terrible struggle, the Turks yielded and began to fall back.

Immediately, the Sultan sent a second wave, personally led by Mustapha Pasha, one of the greatest Ottoman generals. For two hours the battle raged on the walls, but the knights held. When the Turks finally withdrew, the ground was almost completely covered by their dead and wounded. Miraculously, the knights had lost only three dead along with an unspecified number of militia.

The disconcerted Sultan then unleashed a continuous bombardment for three straight weeks. On September 24, another great assault was hurled against the crumbling fortress walls. The bastion of Aragon, one of the city's main fortifications, fell to a massive assault by the now fanatically brave Janissaries, having born the humiliation from their previous defeat for more than forty years. Like Xerxes, Suleiman had a conqueror's throne set on a raised platform so that he could witness his day of triumph. The tide of battle roared all along the walls as wave after wave of Turks poured out of their trenches.

The Turks assumed that it would end quickly, but all day long the battle continued to rage. The knights, in their gleaming armor, always seemed to appear wherever the fighting was the thickest. L'Isle Adam himself could usually be found with his standard bearer behind him at the most desperate points of conflict. He was the man the Turks most wanted killed, and his standard bearer seemed to mark him as the special target. Yet, it was witnessed by those present that there was a special protection around the Grand Master that the Turks simply could not penetrate. After one of the bloodiest days the great Turkish army would ever experience, the seemingly invincible attack began to waver, then melt into a wholesale retreat.

The disbelieving Suleiman came down from his elevated throne humiliated and outraged. He immediately condemned his two most able generals, but later recanted after being persuaded that it would only serve the side of the Christians. The losses for the knights had been great, with two hundred killed and an equal number wounded, but the losses for the Turks were staggering—their bodies now laid in heaps all around the city. Again, the great siege guns were brought up and would not fall silent again for two entire months.

The gallant knights had stood their ground against the most powerful and determined army on earth for nearly five months without receiving reinforcements or provisions. They were now few and weary, and it was obvious to all that the Turkish army was still so huge that it would eventually prevail. Still they fought on, their greatest hope now was only to die honorably.

THE SULTAN'S BENEVOLENCE

As the siege wore on, the Sultan's disposition toward the Order gradually began to change. He respected honor and courage, and had never witnessed the kind of valor that these brave knights had displayed. On Christmas Eve, Suleiman made an extraordinary offer of peace with honor to the remaining knights. He paid tribute to their courage and endurance. He gave them provisions and his own ships to carry them to the destination of their choice. After meeting with L'Isle Adam, Suleiman is reported to have said to his Grand Vizir, "It saddens me to be compelled to force this brave old man to leave his home."

Two thousand men had taken their stand against as many as two hundred thousand, and had held their ground for more than six months. They endured possibly the greatest bombardment and infantry assaults that the world had seen until that time. When hearing the news of the final fall of Rhodes, Charles V of France stated that, "Nothing in the world was ever so well lost as Rhodes." The knights who had already gained the respect of the entire world were now esteemed even more highly. Even so, some of the greatest exploits of the Order were yet to come.

THE KNIGHTS OCCUPY MALTA

For more than two hundred years the knights had lived on Rhodes and now they had no home. They were offered a small, relatively inhospitable island in the middle of the Mediterranean named Malta. They accepted it with gratitude. Years before, while harbored on a ship at Malta, lightening had struck the sword of L'Isle Adam, turning it to ashes. This was to be considered a providential sign. The knights were destined to fight yet another one of history's most strategic battles on the bluffs around that very harbor.

With Rhodes in his possession, the Sultan now seemed free to sweep across the rest of Europe. It seemed most improbable that the battered knights would again bar his path. However, even though the Order of St. John was severely reduced in both numbers and wealth, their most valuable possession—resolve—was as great as ever.

At the same time, Christian Europe had not only failed to resolve its internal divisions, the Reformation had caused the resentment toward Rome to boil over into terrible wars as Christians took up arms against each other. Almost every nation in Europe was at war to some degree with at least one neighbor. Even though the Order of St. John was composed of knights from the noble families of every Christian nation, they were able to maintain remarkable unity, mostly because they remained focused on what they considered to be the real enemy of the faith—the hoards of Islam. As soon as the knights occupied Malta they began building fortifications and ships so that they could resume raiding Moslem shipping. The famous Arab pirate, Barbarossa, had been appointed High Admiral of the Turkish fleet, and he raised its quality and strength to new heights. Great sea battles raged from one end of the Mediterranean to the other. Though most of these battles were indecisive they kept the world on the edge of its seat.

In 1546, Barbarossa died and Dragut assumed command of the increasingly powerful Turkish navy. In 1550, the knights were major participants in the defeat of his fleet at Mahdia. For revenge, Dragut attacked and began to lay waste to Malta. Still relatively unfortified, the few defenders put up such a stiff resistance that Dragut abandoned the attack, but both sides knew that the Turks would soon return.

In 1557, L'Isle Adam died and Jean Parisot De La Valette became Grand Master of the Order. Also educated and aristocratic, La Valette was once captured by the Turks and had been made a galley slave for four years. He was sixty-three when he became Grand Master. He would prove to be as great a leader as both L'Isle Adam and d'Aubusson who had been before him. Suleiman had now stretched his empire to its greatest limits and was massing for what appeared to be the final assault on Europe. But again the knights had to be dealt with because they were creating such havoc with his supply lines, even though they were fewer in numbers and farther away.

THE BATTLE OF MALTA

The whole Moslem world was now demanding the destruction of the Order of St. John. The Sultan was ambivalent. At times he was enraged at the knights, and at times he feared them, knowing that they could not be defeated without great cost. Public opinion soon forced his hand and on May 18, 1565, the Turkish fleet was sighted by the watchman in Fort St. Elmo on the edge of Malta.

The Moslem fleet was so large that witnesses said that it appeared as if an entire forest of spars were moving across the Mediterranean. In fact, the world had never witnessed a more powerful fleet assembled. Again, tens of thousands of the Sultan's finest Janissaries, regulars, and over 4,000 Layalars, religious fanatics who sought death over life, landed to give battle to the 540 knights, 1,000 foot soldiers, and a little more than 3,000 Maltese militia.

Again the Order faced seemingly impossible odds, but even worse they also faced a much more determined foe. The knights did not have enough men to hold the invaders at their beachhead. However, unlike Rhodes where there was just one fortified city, at Malta the knights were spread out over several forts and fortified cities that forced the Turks to diversify their forces. La Valette quickly proved to be a genius at taking the maximum advantage of every favorable condition. He sent the Order's cavalry to attack and harass the Turkish foraging parties. This became such a distraction that it disrupted the unity of Moslem forces.

The Turkish High Command was again led by the brilliant and determined Mustapha Pasha. However, he immediately made a strategic mistake of concentrating his main attack on the Post of Castile, possibly the strongest of the knight's defenses. This was the result of the bravery of a single knight, a Frenchman named Adrien de la Riviere, who had been captured by the Ottomans. Under torture, de la Riviere had asserted that the Post of Castile was lightly fortified with a small garrison of men, and could be easily taken. After a number of assaults were repulsed and mauled by the Post of Castile's defenders, Pasha realized that he had been lied to by the captured knight. He had the Frenchman beaten to death but he had already lost hundreds of his fighters and even more importantly, his troops had already begun to lose confidence.

ST. ELMO'S FIRE

Then Pasha redirected the main part of his force to capturing the small star fort, St. Elmo, which overlooked the Grand Harbor. This too worked in the favor of the knights giving La Valette time to make improvements in his other fortifications. However, no one expected St. Elmo to hold out long. The indiscriminate gunfire of the Turk's earlier sieges at Rhodes had now been replaced by mathematical precision and accuracy. Pasha turned his main artillery on St. Elmo with unrelenting intensity day and night. Soon the little fort began to crumble.

One night, while in his counsel chamber in Fort St. Angelo, La Valette was disturbed by an unwelcome delegation. A number of knights had slipped out of St. Elmo and made their way to La Valette to tell him that St. Elmo could no longer hold out. La Valette, a hero at Rhodes, derided the younger knights as unworthy of their fathers. He told the delegation that they need not go back to St. Elmo, but that he would hand pick knights to relieve them. Under this scorn, the delegation from St. Elmo begged to be allowed to return to their post, which La Valette finally permitted. As soon as they had departed, the Grand Master told the council that he knew that the little fort was doomed, but they had to buy more time if the rest were to have any chance to survive.

The Turks had now concentrated so much artillery on St. Elmo that the smoke and fire rising from the fort made it appear like a volcano rising out of the rock. It seemed impossible that anyone could live in it, but the young knights held their ground. Then the famed Dragut arrived with a fresh squadron of ships, and thousands more of Islam's best fighting men. This greatly raised the morale of the entire Turkish force.

Dragut unofficially assumed personal command of the forces, and he immediately sent even more batteries to pour their deadly fire into St. Elmo, which he continued for three more weeks. Finally he released the Janissaries to make their attack. The commanders on both sides, who had been certain that Turks would make it a quick victory, were equally astonished when the mighty Janissaries were repulsed with heavy losses.

The enraged Dragut then responded with a bombardment so intense that the entire island shook as if by an earthquake. The next day he sent a second massive assault against the little fort with the Layalars preceding the Janissaries. St. Elmo disappeared under the cloud of dust, smoke, and fire. Hours later when the smoke cleared, the knights on St. Angelo and St. Michaels marveled as they saw the Cross of St. John still flying above the crumbled ruins. La Valette was so moved that he dispatched some of his best fighters to reinforce the little fort, but the Moslem forces encircling it could not be penetrated, and they had to turn back. The brave little garrison at St. Elmo was now abandoned to its own fate.

The following day Dragut intensified the bombardment of St. Elmo. There were now fewer than one hundred knights left in the fort and nearly all were wounded. When the bombardment stopped, the Imams were heard calling the faithful to either conquer or die for Islam. Wave after wave of the best fighters in the Sultan's army threw themselves at the demolished walls of the fort. The remaining knights took their stand in the breach; those who were too weak to stand asked to be carried into the fray so that they could confront the "infidels" one last time. It was their last.

The little fortress that no one believed could hold out more than a day or two, stood for more than a month, buying precious time for the rest of the knights to strengthen their other defenses. Little St. Elmo also deprived the Sultan of thousands of his best fighting men, many of his leaders, including the master gunner, the Aga of the Janissaries, and most importantly, Dragut himself who was felled by a cannon shot.

As the Moslem standard was finally raised over the ruins of St. Elmo, Pasha realized that his whole strategy had been wrong. The price paid for St. Elmo had been too dear. As he looked up at the larger St. Angelo, whose guns were already pouring a deadly fire into his advancing troops, he cried out, "Allah! If so small a son has cost so dear, what price shall we have to pay for so large a father?" The price would be greater than he could afford.

No Quarter Given

Pasha had the bodies of the knights who had died so bravely at St. Elmo, decapitated, bound to crosses, and floated out into the harbor in front of St. Angelo. This was a brazen insult to the religion of the defenders. In retaliation, La Valette had a number of the Turkish prisoners executed and their bodies hung on the walls. He then had their heads loaded into cannons and fired into the Moslem trenches. Both sides now knew that there could be no turning back. The knights would survive on Malta or they would perish to a man—this was a fight to the death.

The bombardments increased as the Order's fortresses were now caught in a deadly crossfire. Intermittently, Pasha would release massive ground assaults at different points of the defenses, seeking just a single breach. Each one resulted in a massacre of his forces. At one point, Pasha maneuvered his troops until they encircled La Valette's own headquarters. He then released a bombardment so great that the inhabitants of the islands of Syracuse and Catania, one hundred seventy miles away, heard the roar of the guns. Before the guns had even stopped, Pasha sent a colossal attack swarming over the walls.

ANOTHER MIRACLE

The Turks finally made a breach and poured into it. A mighty struggle raged for six hours until the knights closed the gap and retook the walls. Mortified, Pasha pulled out his own beard and called off the attack. Again, the endurance and tenacity of the knights had been greatly underestimated.

Pasha intensified his bombardment and continued it day and night for seven more days. Then he released another human wave assault. By now the Order was so reduced in numbers that the breach was made quickly. The knights resisted bravely but they were too outnumbered to stand against so great a tide of raging humanity. Just when the citadel itself was within reach of the Turks, and it was obvious that the end of the knights had finally come, the Moslem trumpets rang out calling for a full scale retreat!

The defenders could only believe that the continent had finally sent them relief. What in fact happened was that a small force of the Order's cavalry had attacked the Moslem base camp at Marsa. The little detachment had struck with such determination and had created so much havoc that they had been mistaken for a much larger force. Fearing an attack from the rear, Pasha had been forced to call a retreat. When he finally learned how he had been deceived right at the very moment when victory was within his grasp, his rage knew no bounds. He redoubled his efforts and released a continuous day and night bombardment on the remaining knights under which it seemed impossible for any living thing to survive.

NO RETREAT

The council of knights recommended that a withdrawal be made from all of the outposts into the single fortress of St. Angelo. La Valette adamantly refused. Military historians agree that his tenacity to hold to this strategy probably saved the knights because it kept the Turks from massing at a single point. La Valette received a dispatch from Don Garcia of Sicily promising to send a relief force of 16,000 men. La Valette was unimpressed. Having received many such promises before, he did not put his trust in princes. He renewed his vow to contest every parcel of Christian ground to the death before he would surrender it to the Turks.

Pasha had not only been pouring their deadly fire into the city over its walls, he had been spending weeks making tunnels under the walls. On August 18, a mine exploded under the Post of Castile and a great breach was made. The Grand Master himself, now seventy years old, grabbed a helmet and his sword and rushed out boldly to meet the attack. The knights and the townspeople, encouraged by his example, picked up any weapon that they could find and flung themselves into the breach with him. La Valette was wounded but refused to retreat. He pointed his sword at the Turkish banners and declared, "Never will I withdraw as long as those banners wave in the wind." The knights again repulsed the mighty Turks.

By now dissensions began to arise within the ranks of the Turkish High Command. The siege of the Order's defenses that had been projected to take no more than a few days had again lasted months, and still there was no end in sight. Pasha started calculating how he could get enough supplies from Tripoli, Greece, or Constantinople to keep up the siege through the winter.

Then, on September 6, Don Garcia's fleet arrived with 8,000 reinforcements for the knights. Even though 8,000 was not a significant number compared to the still huge army of the Turks, their impact on the morale of both sides was much greater than their numbers. The Turks were simply appalled when they considered what just a few hundred knights had cost them. They had still only captured the little fort of St. Elmo, so how could they possibly prevail against so many more? Pasha lifted the siege, struck camp, and fled the island.

The Sultan's grand army returned to the Golden Horn with less than one third of those who had left. Suleiman was once again enraged. He only allowed the fleet to come into the harbor under the cover of darkness so that the people would not see its terrible state. He immediately began planing to lead another expedition to Malta, but like Mehmet before him, Suleiman would not live to fulfill this vow.

EUROPE CELEBRATES

Only about 250 knights survived the Battle of Malta. Every one of them had been wounded. Many had been maimed, or crippled for life. Even so, Europe was now free of the Moslem threat that had so recently appeared invincible. Again the world stood in wonder at the little Order of St. John the Baptist. Those "archaic relics from the past" had taken their stand against the most powerful army on the earth, and with some of the greatest examples of courage and endurance the world had ever seen, they had prevailed.

The great monarchs of Europe who had so recently scorned the Order of St. John acknowledged that these few brave souls had saved them from Moslem conquest. Queen Elizabeth declared that if Malta had fallen to the Turks, England itself would have almost certainly one day fallen to the Moslems. She ordered the Archbishop of Canterbury to appoint a special form of thanksgiving to be read in every church in the land every day for three weeks. The rest of Europe also celebrated, paying their respects and acknowledging their debt to the Order that so many had written off as having no real value. The Order's standard with the famous Maltese Cross would become for a time the only standard to be saluted by every nation recognized on earth. Even the Moslem nations honored them for their courage and tenacity. Some nations still observe St. John's Day to celebrate the exploits of these valiant knights.

THE LESSONS

There are many great and timely lessons in the amazing history of the Order of St. John, but here we will only address the most basic. Great strategists have often changed the course of humanity, but these knights were not great strategists—they were simply great souls. Their resolve, courage, and endurance accomplished what possibly no great strategy could have. Sometimes leadership is reduced to simple resolve, and in this, leadership often finds its greatest definition. Neither can leadership be overly focused on the odds, or the resources available. Great leaders stay focused on the task, and do the best that they can with what they have.

The Order of St. John also demonstrated what can be accomplished when there is unity. While the Christian nations of Europe had turned their armies against each other, the knights of St. John stayed focused on who the real threat was to their faith. Even though the Order was composed of the noble sons of those Christian nations that were fighting each other, they did not allow the doctrinal or political divisions to enter their ranks. Because of their unity, focused vision, and determination never to retreat before their enemies, they dramatically turned back what had appeared to be the inevitable course of history. It is now almost impossible to imagine what history would have been like without these few brave souls.

THE PRESENT STATUS OF THE ORDER

As I am constantly asked this question, I will address it briefly here. The Order's resiliency and ability to survive is almost as amazing as their great military exploits. It is today possibly the only true chivalrous Order in existence that has maintained legitimate, continuous roots to the Crusades. Committed to honor, the defense of the faith, Christian unity, and service to "my lords the sick and the poor," the "knights of Malta" as they are now called, are still involved in some of the most extraordinary diplomatic breakthroughs of recent times, albeit without fanfare or any attempts to be recognized.

Just like the church, there are now both ecumenical and Catholic divisions of the Order, with some natural contention between them as to which are the true heirs. There are also a host of other smaller groups who now claim to be the true heirs of the Order, but if the right of survivorship test had to be passed, then the ecumenical Sovereign Order of St. John the Baptist, of Jerusalem, Rhodes, and Malta seems to have the most legitimate claim, because the Catholic Order became dormant until resuscitated and a new Grand Mastership was recognized by Pope Leo XIII in 1879.

Even so, both the ecumenical and Catholic Orders do have legitimate and substantial claims to the Order's history and both are recognized in many nations. The Catholic Grand Master holds the rank of Cardinal in the church. Ecumenical branches of the Order now exist in Canada, Ireland, Germany, Sweden, France, Rhodes, Austria, Australia, Switzerland, Belgium, Portugal, Spain, Italy, Greece, China, The Netherlands, and the United States. Entry into the ecumenical Order can only be attained by qualification and recommendation by a present member. There are no secret rites or customs involved but simple compliance with the highest standards of Christian faith, morality, integrity, and unity. Entry into the Catholic Order also requires allegiance to the Roman Catholic Church.

CHAPTER FIFTEEN

THE FIVE ESSENTIALS FOR SUCCESS IN MANAGEMENT

Previously, we discussed the five essentials for success in leadership. Here we are going to discuss the five essentials required for success in the management of any enterprise. Understanding and applying these five basic essentials is the key to solid, secure success. They are: 1) The Product, 2) Administration, 3) Marketing, 4) Resources, 5) Timing.

Whether it is a business, church, army, sports team, or even a government, for the effective management of any enterprise these five essentials must be understood and combined to work in harmony and support of each other. Failure to understand, control, and keep these essentials in proper balance can be found as the reason for almost every failure in the history of human enterprise.

We can have any four of these essentials working perfectly but if the other one is ineffective it can destroy the entire venture. For example, we can have a quality Product, perfect Timing for its release, great Administration, and plenty of Resources, but poor Marketing can make all of our efforts fruitless. We can have the perfect Product, Administration, Timing, and Marketing, but a lack of Resources can be our doom. Combine any four of the essentials successfully but neglect the other one, and we will be in jeopardy of ultimate failure.

Once we understand these five essentials, it is easy to comprehend why the majority of new businesses fail in their first year of existence. Of those that survive the first year, only a fraction will survive three more. Many great new products never succeed in the marketplace simply because they were not backed by strength in just one of these five basic essentials. Of those that do survive many just limp along falling short of their real potential because they do not get these basics under control and functioning properly.

Our goal in this study is to impart basic principles that can be understood and applied quickly, simply, and easily for success. Once we understand the mechanics and interrelationship of these five essentials, the effectiveness of management will be greatly enhanced.

MANAGING FOR RESULTS

The goal of effective management should always be clarity and simplicity, which gets *results.* The gravitation to esoteric management principles and theories is nothing more than a cloak for the basic lack of understanding by those who generate them. With few exceptions the greatest leaders and most effective managers have all been committed to understanding and applying the *basics* in their field of enterprise.

Commitment to excellence will only go as deep as our commitment to the philosophy of excellence. Only when we do the right things for the right reasons will our commitment be deep enough to accomplish our potential for true and lasting success. Consequently, philosophy as well as the practical application of these principles must be considered.

With just a basic understanding of the application of the five essentials, we can quickly and effectively discern, and possibly compensate for, weakness in one or more of the other essentials for a period of time. A weakness in a competitor or enemy can also be easily discerned in this way. The goal of our understanding must be to have all of the essentials working in harmony like a finely tuned machine while being able to judge weakness or opportunity, so that these strengths can be used effectively.

To give a brief illustration of how easy it is to analyze almost any project, mission, or enterprise with the five essentials, let's use them to superficially dissect three entirely different enterprises: a professional football team, an army, and a business.

MANAGING A TEAM

The game is the Product of the football team. If it can produce a quality game, it has a quality Product. The coaching, recruiting, and front office would be the Administration. Marketing would be all of the efforts to promote attendance at the games, an interest in the sport, etc. Resources would be the talent of the players and staff as well as the capital required to acquire them. *Timing is the fundamental essential which is vital for the success of all the other essentials.*

For the football team, the proper use of Timing is quite obvious in the game (Product), calling the right plays at the right time, etc., but it is just as essential in every other department. Promotions will be most effective if released in early fall when people start thinking about football. They will probably have little effect if released in early spring when people start thinking about the lazy days of summer and the more appropriate laidback game of baseball. Administration will have the consideration of Timing as the basis for making most of its decisions. For example, knowing the age and health of their present players should determine *when* they should draft or recruit players for those positions. A continually successful team will be strong and consistent in all five of the essentials.

Using the five essentials to discern the strengths and weaknesses of other teams can play a big part in our team's strategy and planning as well. Knowing that our competitor's Product is strong in pass defense, but weak in running defense may cause us to consider giving more attention to our running game so we can exploit their weaknesses and avoid their strengths. If our main competition is weak in capitalization, we might need to consider outbidding them for the quality free agents. Knowing our strengths and weaknesses, as well as those of the competition, will enable us to formulate a more effective strategy.

MANAGING AN ARMY

Now let's look at the army. Its ability to wage battle would be its Product. Its Administration would include the commanding general down to the corporal directing a squad. Marketing would be its ability to recruit and maintain public opinion to encourage the civilian sacrifice required for success (Marketing had as much to do with the Allied victory in World War II as field strategy). Its Resources would be the men, arms, and supplies available. Timing would be involved in knowing when to attack where and with what weapons, as well as when and how to strengthen certain defenses.

Near the end of World War II, the German army still had a quality Product (ability to fight), effective Administration on the battlefield, effective Marketing in promoting the sacrifice required by their population, and almost perfect Timing in initiating the Battle of the Bulge—but the lack of Resources (they ran out of fuel) sealed their defeat. The Allied army's discernment of this German weakness helped them implement a successful defensive strategy. They simply let the Germans advance until their fuel ran out (which created the *bulge*), exploiting this weakness until they attained the ultimate victory.

History testifies that it is poor Timing to invade Russia unless you can get your army out before the winter. Napoleon invaded Russia with overwhelming strength in every essential except Timing. Even though the French had adequate Resources when they initiated the invasion, their Timing opened a door of vulnerability to the discerning Russians. They could not beat Napoleon on the battlefield so they burned their cities and fields to deprive him of the Resources he was counting on to survive the winter. Through this strategy of attacking Napoleon's only area of weakness, the Russians utterly destroyed one of the most invincible armies ever assembled.

MANAGING A BUSINESS

In considering a business, its Product would be the product(s), or service(s) offered. Its Administration would be the management from its board of directors down to the most junior foreman. Marketing would include its promotions and distribution. Resources would include its capitalization, the necessary people, machines, or factories, as well as whatever natural resources are needed to make the Product. Again, Timing is the hub around which the other spokes are joined. We could build the best quality and least expensive hula-hoop ever made, but if we did not get it out in the 1950s we probably missed our chance.

Piper and Cessna aircraft manufacturers built comparable Products. Both companies had good Administration, adequate Resources, and good Timing for their Products. Everything else being about equal, Cessna sold many times the number of aircrafts that Piper did simply because they were stronger in Marketing.

Ford Motor Company started off with the best Product, Timing, Resources, and Marketing, but was a little weak in Administration. General Motors started with strength in Administration but was behind in the other Essentials. At first GM could do little more than copy Ford products and patiently wait for Ford to make a mistake. Ford left an opening in Product development and Timing. Ford produced the same Model T year after year while GM started improving their Product each year. Through strong Marketing, GM made new cars a fad and Ford's Product obsolete, thereby seizing the initiative in the automotive industry, which they would not relinquish for decades. Had Ford been monitoring all of the five essentials in his enterprise along with those of his competitor, he would never have fallen behind GM. Had GM been monitoring the five essentials in its enterprise along with its competitors, GM probably would not have lost its leadership to the Japanese which discerned the trend toward the smaller size and higher quality long before Detroit perceived it.

These are just cursory examples of how an enterprise can be dissected into the five essential parts to be more quickly and effectively examined for its strengths and weaknesses. Of course, there will be some variations to these essentials in every different enterprise. However, generally these principles will be applicable and useful in developing and managing almost any venture.

SPINNING PLATES

There will be a constant shifting of emphasis to shore up one or more of these five essentials to maintain a balance in those enterprises that survive and prosper. For example, when major corporations make a change in their Chief Executive Officer, the board will most often use the change to strengthen the essentials, which are showing weakness. If Marketing is weak they will bring in someone strong in that area. However, those in Marketing will often have little understanding of engineering or product development, so the Product may tend to suffer while the main emphasis is on Marketing.

Then with the next change they will bring someone in to strengthen the weakened Product, and the Marketing may begin to weaken again. Seldom is there to be found an enterprise that maintains constant harmony in all of the essential areas. Like clowns spinning plates at the circus—they get one group going and the others start to wobble.

Fortunately, with a better understanding of these basics it is possible to have all of the essentials doing well at the same time. For a truly healthy and lasting enterprise this is crucial. Many businesses that have failed would not have done so if they had understood and applied these principles. Some may have closed their businesses, understanding that their time was over, but they could have been closed in victory instead of defeat and ruin.

Understanding these simple principles can lay a solid foundation for insight and foresight, both of which are necessary for success. In the following chapters we will draw from many different enterprises for examples to instill creativity in the application of this principle so it can be easily applied to your situation.

SIMPLICITY IN DIVERSITY

With insight, and imagination, we can literally see how Napoleon's battle plans will help us in the shop or on the farm. Our situation at the factory or at the law firm may sometimes require just as much courage, determination, and brilliance as the most celebrated coaches if we are going to succeed. The basics for all of us are essentially the same. They apply to the largest corporation, government, or to the smallest individual proprietor.

Napoleon used the principle of the five essentials in all of his military planning. He measured his army's fighting strategies and improved them (the Product). He trained his officers to think strategically, and motivated them with his vision (Administration). He was a master at raising needed capital, troops, and supplies (Resources). His vision and leadership inspired France and sometimes even the citizens of enemy nations (Marketing), and he consistently used Timing as one of his most powerful weapons. He failed in the invasion of Russia and at Waterloo because of his disregard for Timing. That is usually the first essential element that we will disregard when we become arrogant or complacent.

Captain Rostron's demonstration of leadership and preparedness as Captain of the Carpathia during the Titanic tragedy was aided by his mastery of the five essentials. He knew his Product well (the ship). He knew and used his Administration and Resources brilliantly. He was a master of Timing and he conveyed his plan so well (Marketing) that his passengers and crew were utterly focused on the task. He knew his ship and his team well enough to quickly and effectively analyze his limitations and possibilities in the midst of changing circumstances and crisis.

General Lee's use of the five essentials while commanding the Army of Northern Virginia is a profound study in this theme. He was able to take full advantage of the essentials, which were strong to overcome those that were weak. He used a fundamental understanding of this principle to know his opponents better than they knew themselves. This kind of insight is both a gift and a discipline to be developed. "You can't put in what God has left out," but we must also develop what God has put in or we have "buried our talents" just as He warned.

An entire volume could easily be devoted to each of these essentials, but for the sake of brevity and simplicity we will devote only a chapter to each. I am not trying to be comprehensive, just effective in imparting easy-to-use principles that work.

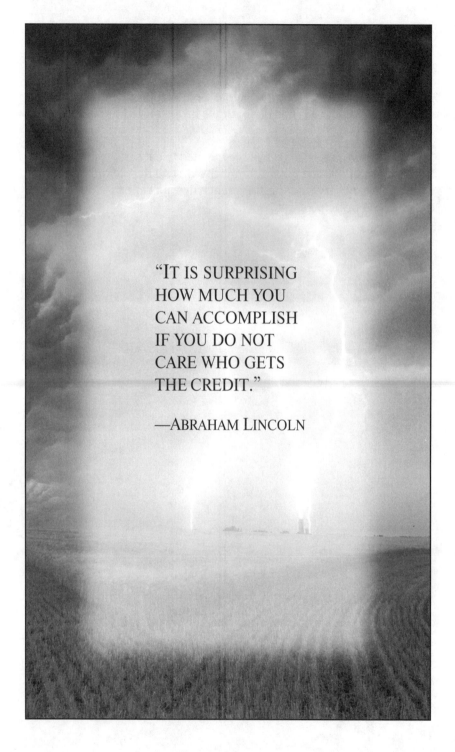

"IT IS SURPRISING
HOW MUCH YOU
CAN ACCOMPLISH
IF YOU DO NOT
CARE WHO GETS
THE CREDIT."

—ABRAHAM LINCOLN

CHAPTER SIXTEEN
THE PRODUCT

The Product is the *reason* for the enterprise—it is what we *produce*. It can be a commodity, a service, even an idea, but it must be kept as the reason for the enterprise. If anything supplants the Product as the primary reason for the enterprise, the slide into mediocrity or failure will begin.

Profit is what usually supplants the Product as the reason for the enterprise. This is not to say that profit should not be *a* motive for the venture, but it should never be *the* motive. Detroit ruled the automotive world when it was motivated by a love for cars. When the finance men gained control of Detroit and changed the emphasis to profit, American leadership in that industry began its decline. These finance men were needed by the industry to increase efficiency but it was a mistake to allow them to take control. They reduced a great art to *mere manufacturing* which is contrary to the soul of America.

America's soul is linked closely to conquest and adventure. This is not an imperialistic type of conquest; it is more the desire to achieve, to push back the outer limits. Without a vision for conquering limits we become bored and our performance falls. Americans will excel at manufacturing only if the process somehow identifies the enterprise with breaking new barriers, not just fattening the bottom line. Profit alone is a superficial and an uninspiring goal to the work force, which is a critical key to success.

MAINTAINING OUR FIRST LOVE

Henry Ford may have impacted the world as much as any other man in modern history. He advanced manufacturing to the point where the modernization that has swept the world was possible. His vision was fired by a love for the car and the desire to make it cheaper and available to more people. But Henry Ford fell from grace by becoming more captivated by the process of making the car than the car itself. He kept tweaking the assembly line to make it faster and more efficient and we all benefited from this, *but he forgot to continue improving the car.*

General Motors (GM) easily copied Ford's manufacturing improve-ments but also strove to make better cars. Little, unknown GM quickly surpassed Ford and for a very long time dominated the industry. GM did not forget why they were in manufacturing, at least until the accountants gained control. When you lose your first love the process of growing has stopped and the process of dying has started.

We may be a manufacturer of the most mundane, insignificant widget there is, but we must not ever think of it as such. If it is worth making, it is important, worth being proud of, and it *can be* an inspiration to our people. Remember Martin Luther King's exhortation, "...If you sweep streets then sweep streets like Michelangelo painted. If you're the best at what you do, even if it's sweeping streets, the whole world will beat a path to your door and declare that 'Here lives the best street sweeper that ever lived'." As King Solomon put it, "The skilled craftsman will not stand before obscure men, but will sit in the presence of kings." It does not matter what you do; if you do it with all of your heart, day in and day out, you will inspire those around you, and there is little that can prevent you from rising to the top.

Regardless of how good your Product is and how much it wins over the competition, by always seeking to improve it, you are sending a powerful message to every little corner of your enterprise. This attitude can do more for affecting company loyalty than fat bonuses.

Every individual's job is his own personal Product. Every Product must be esteemed as important because that makes every person important. This means more to them than just about anything else you can offer. If every individual's Product is important, then the overall Product of the enterprise is that much more so. Regardless of your position in the enterprise, faithfulness to this concept ensures your success and makes you a true leader. If you are a leader and your enterprise is composed of leaders, your Product is almost assured of leading its field.

TWO GREAT LEADERS

After leaving the service, I spent a couple of years learning the carpenter trade. I had the privilege of working with a great craftsman we knew simply as "Old Joe." At that time the country was in a severe recession. One day I remarked how so many in our trade were being hurt by it. He objected and declared that: "No good carpenters are ever hurt by recession." He saw recession as bringing a healthy pruning of the trade, an opportunity to purge the pretenders.

This old man had been through the depression and a multitude of recessions and hardly knew they were happening because he built houses like Michelangelo painted. He took three young men and inspired such a love for carpentry in us that we were disappointed to see five o'clock come each day because it meant we had to stop. At night we couldn't wait for the next morning so we could get started again. We did great work but we were always trying to do even better.

I have met quite a few important leaders, but few ever impressed me as much as that old carpenter. I will always remember him as a great man and a great leader. His Product made him great. Every man is ultimately known by his Product. Is this not what Jesus meant when He said, "By their fruits you will know them?" Every man is ultimately known by what he produces and leaves behind.

A few years later I became a flight instructor and I considered myself one of the great American pilots. I then met a pilot named Joe Logan. He owned North American Aircraft Delivery, and was a world renowned aircraft ferry pilot. He had flown over one hundred small, single engine aircraft across the Atlantic to such places as Saudi Arabia and South Africa. Israel, who was considered to have some of the best military pilots in the world actually hired Joe to train some of them.

On my first flight with Joe I determined that I was going to teach him a few things about flying. We were hardly off the ground before he was in my face screaming about my lack of smoothness. In just a few more minutes he seized the controls claiming that I was trying to throw him out of his seat! After I got over my anger I began to watch him fly. Soon I felt that I did not even deserve to be a private pilot, much less a commercial pilot and flight instructor. I had never seen such precision and knowledge of the air and the aircraft. I went on to train pilots for their airline ratings, and worked with some who were considered top fighter pilots, but I never met another one as good as Joe. One day he shared his secret with me.

Ferrying aircraft is where the saying came from that flying was many hours of boredom occasionally interrupted by moments of sheer terror. However, Joe determined on one of his first flights that he was not going to just sit there and watch the gauges while the autopilot did all the work—he was going to use this time to become the best pilot that he could. Joe flew those missions by hand and he kept score on himself. He would put a clipboard in the cockpit and whenever he deviated from the course more than five degrees, or from his altitude by more than fifty feet, or even slightly felt any "G" forces during a maneuver indicating a lack of precision, he would put a mark on the board.

The first few times when he reached his destination he would have several hundred marks on the board. Most pilots would consider that a great score under the circumstances. Many pilots would have considered it a great score just to get there! Joe determined that every time he got in the cockpit he was not only going to improve his score, he was going to be a better pilot. On one of his last trips he had just two marks on the board and he still was not satisfied! No one knew or cared about this but Joe. He was simply determined to be the best pilot that he could be.

YOUR PRODUCT IS YOU

Your Product is an extension of your soul; it is a reflection of who you are. If you run a large corporation then everything it does is *you*. If you run a small shop by yourself, your work is *you*. If you are the assistant to the janitor, you can inspire everyone in the company by your devotion to excellence. If you are a housewife you can instill greatness and a focused leadership vision in your whole family by how you manage your home. There is a great biblical truth that states—*you will reap what you sow*. If you are tireless in doing the best you can do you will ultimately be rewarded.

THE FOUNDATION OF GREATNESS

A fundamental reason for the early failure of business is that many go into business just to be their own boss. That is not a good reason for starting an enterprise and will seldom provide the motivation to endure the problems and obstacles required to succeed. There is something in most of us that rebels at the thought of just being average. Those who are not striving to rise above the status quo usually spend most of their free time dreaming about it. However, if we really want our lives to be significant the delusion that seeking greatness will ever make us great must be dispelled. Those who have left their imprint on human history did so because they were focused on something beyond themselves—they were focused on the Product.

Those who just seek greatness are self-centered. When the self-centered and self-important gain influence or power they become the tyrants and scourges of history. The self-seeking and self-important inevitably become petty and insignificant.

True greatness only comes when a person concentrates his love and attention on something beyond himself. For Moses, it was freeing men from slavery so that they could be released for true worship. For Socrates, it was understanding. For Michelangelo it was painting that gave expression to truth. For Tolstoy it was literature that gave expression to truth. For Einstein it was science that explained the "Reason that manifests itself in nature." For Jesus it was to give men redemption from their failures and delusions so they could know God and attain the stature and majesty for which He had created them. Everyone who has had a positive impact on human history has given more importance to the purpose or Product than to personal fulfillment. To have a single focus upon something beyond ourselves, something that is greater than ourselves, has the power to turn even the mundane into a powerful vehicle of human advancement.

Whatever is worth doing is worth doing well. We may start doing it poorly, but we must determine that we will do it as well as it can be done. Whatever is worth our top priority is worth doing with all of our hearts. Greatness does not result from wanting to be great, but by the determination to take something outside of ourselves to greater heights. Regardless of who we are, and what level of human esteem and position we now hold, by identifying our Product and making it the focus of our attention and effort, we will make a difference. The one who takes a mediocre task and raises it to the level of significance is an artist who deserves the world's attention as a great leader.

THE PRACTICAL PRINCIPLES OF THE PRODUCT

The first step toward making your Product successful is to make it your passion. If you are not in love with your Product, it may be hard for anyone else to even like it. The passion of true love is more contagious than any disease. If you are passionate about your Product, that passion will spread to others. Victor Kiam loved the Remington razor enough to buy the whole company. His entire sales pitch was his passion for that razor, and that passion sold more razors than price or quality had ever been able to sell.

The next principle is to make your Product at least useful, but if possible, to make it essential. There has to be a purpose for the Product. George Washington Carver took the peanut which was on or near the bottom of just about everyone's priority list and made it useful, even essential in some of its discovered applications. George Washington Carver's life is a testimony that, regardless of how insignificant we feel that our Product or Service is, if we are devoted enough we can discover applications that will raise its value and usefulness. Creativity must be applied in making the Product *and* in finding applications for its use.

The next principle for making your Product successful is to price it fairly. The more fair the price, the more successful you will ultimately be. Pricing should be determined by what we *should* get, not what we *could* get. If you take advantage of a present monopoly or critical need for your Product to squeeze all that you can out of those who need it, you may get their present business, but you will not get their future business if they can possibly give it to anyone else. Greed kills when it comes to enterprise. *You can shear a sheep many times, but you can only skin it once.*

If you are now thinking that this is all idealistic, you are right, to a degree. Idealism can be a delusion that can lead to extinction, but a lack of idealism *will* lead to extinction. If you have abandoned all idealism for the sake of gain you have lost your humanity and any potential for significance.

Unfortunately, "the ugly American" is a title earned by many United States businessmen and officials abroad. Not only have we been arrogant and presumptuous, we have tried to compensate for lack of quality and value in our Product by using hype and manipulation. That may work for a little while, but it will always result in ultimate failure.

Just a few decades ago, Americans were esteemed as honest and straightforward individuals who would do business with a handshake. Then a subtle form of legalism crept in to the fiber of the nation and whatever was *legal* was considered to be right. The thought was, if you could get away with it you should do it. If a future historian writes about the rise and fall of America, he will almost certainly discover this subtle but terrible deception to be the ax that felled this great and mighty tree. If we do not make dramatic and substantial changes, "Made in America" will continue to be an epithet for poor quality, overpricing, and dependence upon hype in place of integrity. If you are motivated to do what you can get away with, you are an enemy of humanity. Like Judas, you may have gained your silver but you have lost your soul.

Winston Churchill astutely observed that "If one is not a liberal at twenty he has no heart, but if he is not a conservative by forty he has no mind." But if by forty one has lost his heart, then his mind will not function right either. True integrity is found in the balance between idealism and pragmatism. For a body to function properly it needs both the mind and the heart. The pendulum has often swung too far towards pragmatism. We must return to the ideals of honesty and value, and we must ponder the *purpose* for which we are offering our Product. The world really does want to love and respect Americans but it is up to us to give them a reason to.

"COURAGE FACES FEAR
AND THEREBY MASTERS IT.
COWARDICE REPRESSES
FEAR AND IS THEREBY
MASTERED BY IT."

—MARTIN LUTHER KING, JR.

CHAPTER SEVENTEEN

ADMINISTRATION

The Administration is the brain and nervous system of every enterprise. Through it all the other Essentials are controlled, just like the brain controls all the organs in our body. Regardless of the quality and strength of the other Essentials, if the Administration is not functioning properly, your venture will be like a healthy body with a sick mind—caught somewhere between out of control and useless. However, if the Administration is healthy, it may be able to compensate for even serious problems in the other essential areas.

CONTROL GROWTH OR FIGHT CANCER

Administration is where all enterprises begin. No one has ever started a venture until someone made the decision to do it, and decisions are the function of Administration. After the initial decision to start, most of the attention then usually goes to the Product, Marketing, Resources, and Timing. The Administration of ventures has a tendency to just evolve, coming together piecemeal, born more out of necessity and crisis than quality planning. This kind of haphazard development of such a crucial part of the venture is a major cause of ultimate failures.

If left to form by circumstances without planning, Administration will become a cancer with its greatest devotion being the feeding of itself. It will keep growing until it has sapped the life out of the rest of the enterprise. Management has a way of increasing layer-by-layer until it is inefficient and ineffective becoming more of a burden than the life force it must be for true success.

Many governments are good examples of Administrations, which have gone awry. In 1980, the United States welfare departments had more than one employee for each recipient of benefits! If the welfare of the less fortunate were the priority, this preposterous ratio would never have been allowed. Obviously the promotion of the department became more important than the reason for which it was created.

The Administrations of many corporations are just as unhealthy. So are those of many schools, hospitals, charities, churches, and ministries. Because Administration is the brain and nervous system of the enterprise, if cancer begins to grow here it will be most deadly.

How is this to be avoided? The development and control of our Administration must be given at least as much attention and planning as the other Essentials. This can only be provided by effective, discerning leadership.

THE OVERLOAD: FRIEND OR ENEMY?

An effective leader must be positive in his orientation, but he must know how to say a most important word: "No!" For example: If an Administration is being dictated by crisis management instead of sound planning, it will want to hire more people every time the work load becomes heavy. Our first response to an overload should not be to spend more money or resources to resolve it, but to use the pressure as an opportunity to find better and more efficient ways to do the job. An efficiently managed enterprise will be overloaded part of the time.

There are cycles to almost all activity. If your workload is too much to keep up with one-third of the time, you will likely not have enough to do about one-third of the time as well. The leader must navigate a tolerable median between the overload and the slack periods for maximum efficiency. Overloads can be creative pressures we need to help us improve our systems and strengthen the muscles of our enterprise. Hiring more people or using more resources to resolve the overloads will only increase the fat, which will weaken the heart of the venture.

President Jimmy Carter once proposed a "zero based budget." Under this plan every department in the government would start with a budget of zero at the beginning of each new fiscal year and would then have to justify every dollar it was given. If the leadership had existed to actually implement this program, it would have greatly increased efficiency in the Federal Government. Some safeguards would have been required but something of this nature must be instituted before the weight of our government destroys the supporting economy.

If there is no system for effectively making Administration accountable on a regular basis it will become fat or cancerous. Left alone, the Administration will quickly begin to think and act as though the entire enterprise exists for its benefit instead of the other way around. It takes constant vigilance on the part of leadership to keep this from happening.

THE REWARD FACTOR

In management you will receive what you reward. It may not be what you want or even plan to receive. Many ventures and enterprises even though their emphasis, training, and effort are devoted to efficient management will fail to ever achieve it because they actually reward mediocrity and penalize efficiency. If there is no accountability the most inefficient departments will end up with the most people, the biggest budgets, the most prestige, power, and influence. At the same time, the most efficient department which has kept its staff lean and effective will actually lose influence and reward. If you want an efficient Administration you must reward efficiency and penalize inefficiency and waste.

THE CHIEF EXECUTIVE OFFICER

For simplicity we are using the title CEO as the head of the enterprise. The title used in your organization may be anything from General to Pastor.

The CEO should be a leader, rather than a manager type. He gives direction to the enterprise as to where it is going and the goals that are to be pursued. The best CEO will be concept oriented, and able to grasp the overall picture. However, he must also be able to understand the details or he will be inclined to give unrealistic goals and poor direction, causing confusion instead of inspiration.

The CEO is a lonely position. The opportunities are great but so are the difficulties. He is often the only one who can see the big picture. The managers responsible for the other essentials will usually feel that their departments are the most important in the company, and, to a degree, you want them to all feel that way. This reflects the importance that they give to their job. The CEO must encourage the loyalty of each department head to his department, but also be able to balance the pressure he gets from each in order to stay on course.

To do this the CEO must know where he's going, and have the courage and fortitude to disregard pressures when necessary or take other proper actions.

TENACITY TEMPERED BY FLEXIBILITY

The CEO like the captain of a ship, must know his destination and course for getting there before he leaves port. Almost every plan will still require some changes because every voyage has surprises which are not in the plan. Because of this the captain must be able to adjust for these surprises while staying as close as possible to the intended course. It is easy to lay out the course while you're in port, but it can be far more difficult to re-compute your navigation after a storm or unexpected problems that have taken you far from your planned position.

As the captain you must keep alert. When the storm comes do not allow it to blow you off course. When a person first looks down at a river from an airplane, he is usually surprised by the way the way the river snakes through the countryside, curling and weaving. Rivers usually travel several times over the necessary distance from beginning to end than if they had just gone straight. Why do rivers flow like that? They take the path of least resistance. If you are inclined to allow resistance to change your course, you are going to be traveling many times the necessary distance to get to your intended goal. Most vessels do not have the fuel or resources to go very far from the original plan. Your judgment in this alone may be the difference between success and failure.

As an aircraft pilot, I determined that it was in my interest to become the best one possible. I asked for the toughest and most intimidating instructors and then I would antagonize them into becoming even meaner. I knew that if I could not operate an aircraft properly under their pressure, then there could be emergency situations that I would have trouble coping with. There were days when I would get back from a training flight and never want to see an airplane again. It was humiliating and frustrating but later when I flew into storms that brought me to the very limits of my skills, I thanked the Lord many times for the toughness of those instructors.

Arrogance causes us to become unteachable, whereas humility keeps us continually learning. Training and preparation never end for the great leaders and managers. Preparation and planning will help you make the *best* choices in whatever circumstances you find yourself.

TWO KINDS OF LEADERSHIP

There are two basic approaches to leadership, the aggressive and the conservative, though there may be unlimited variations of each. There are advantages to each of these approaches. With few exceptions, the most renowned leaders in history have been of the extreme aggressive nature. However, the overwhelming majority of successful leaders, though maybe less notable have been the conservative type. The aggressive leaders who can adjust and be conservative when it is appropriate are the most successful of all. Few have achieved this flexibility. Let's briefly look at each type of leader.

THE AGGRESSIVE LEADER

These are the homerun hitters. They almost hate singles and want to swing for the fences every time they come to the plate. Like a homerun, their successes are spectacular. However, when swinging for the fences, you are going to strike out more often. The same attitude that leads to the greatest successes also leads to the most devastating failures. If you are afraid to fail, you will never succeed because you will never really play the game.

The greatest leaders have learned to use their failures as opportunities for reaching even greater heights. We usually learn more from failure than we do from success. Those who attain a degree of success without failure will tend to be superficial and naive. They are easily spotted as the ones who have all the answers. The truly great leaders will be those who would rather listen than talk, always seeking more understanding. Consider this about Abraham Lincoln, one of the greatest leaders ever produced by America:

- He failed in business in 1831
- He was defeated for the Legislature in 1832
- He failed again in business in 1833
- He suffered a nervous breakdown in 1836
- He was defeated for Speaker of the Legislature in 1838
- He was defeated for Elector in 1840
- He was defeated for Congress in 1843
- He was defeated again for Congress in 1848
- He was defeated for the Senate in 1855
- He was defeated for Vice President in 1856

- He was defeated for the Senate again in 1858
- He was elected President in 1860
- He saved the Union

It is hard to comprehend how a man could endure the continual crises and pressures Abraham Lincoln suffered while President. At times he was abandoned by his own party—even his closest friends. But he resolutely held to the course until victory was attained. The list above explains such endurance. The man was well acquainted with failure—but he was never a quitter! Every defeat made Lincoln more determined and prepared for his ultimate task. Setbacks will either make us *better* or they will make us *bitter*, the choice is up to us.

By observing the great championship sports teams, they had many more years that they did not win a championship than when they did. We will learn far more from our failures than from our victories, but we must never become satisfied with failure. When we resign ourselves to failure we become a failure. But if we will use our failures to increase our ultimate resolve, we are destined for victory.

The aggressive category of leader has produced the most renowned and memorable characters in history. Brilliant victories and devastating failures punctuate each of their lives. Austerlitz then Waterloo, Chancelorsville then Gettysburg. They won big and lost big but they played the game with all of their hearts.

Those with this nature would rather lose it all than live any other way. If you are not of this nature, it is almost impossible to understand those who are. They are few in number but the course of history has followed in their wake. If you are one of these or if you work for one, you're in for a wild ride. They live perpetually on the thin line between heartbreaking disaster and breathtaking achievement.

The following are some of the characteristics of the aggressive temperament:

STRENGTHS:

- Seldom discouraged
- Will take charge without hesitation
- Decisive
- Adventurous
- Will not quit

WEAKNESSES:

- Lack compassion, and can be harsh
- Impatient
- Set standards too high, expect too much from others
- Seldom give praise to others
- Impetuous, often make rash decisions
- Will not retreat even when it is strategic and wise
- Tendency to over-commit

THE CONSERVATIVE LEADER

The Conservative leaders are no less important to progress and success. Without them the chaos on earth would probably be unbearable. They provide stability and longevity. Their lives may not be as spectacular as the aggressive types but are usually meaningful and fulfilling. These are often referred to as "the salt of the earth." They may move slower than the aggressive types, but their genius can be just as profound.

General Longstreet, a corporal commander in Lee's Army of Northern Virginia, was of this nature. In many of the successful battles he may have been as responsible for victory as the more famous Stonewall Jackson. He did not move as fast, but neither was he moved from his position quickly. Many historians believe that Longstreet deserved the nickname "Stonewall" more than Jackson, if you look at the whole course of the war. Longstreet was unspectacular but consistent. On one hand his slow movement at Gettysburg may have cost the Confederacy a sweeping victory, and even the war. Even so, had Lee listened to his counsel there would not have been a "Pickett's charge," which did cost them the battle and probably the war.

When the conservative leader loses, it is usually because he fails to take advantage of opportunity. He wins sometimes simply because he is the only one left. If an enterprise can have a partnership of leaders with each of these natures, as the Army of Northern Virginia did while Jackson was alive, it can have the greatest opportunity of all.

After Gettysburg, Lee paid more attention to Longstreet. If you consider the increased odds they were facing, they won some of their most remarkable battles during this time. Some historians claim they never really lost another battle—they just ran out of men and resources.

Longstreet's defensive genius in all of these conflicts is evident. The tactics he devised were actually most used by armies around the world for the next one hundred years. Even so, history does not remember Longstreet as well as it does Lee and Jackson. Seldom will men, or history, give this type of solid leader their due, but they are no less responsible for shaping history or present human affairs.

True wisdom in leadership is to know when to be aggressive and when to be conservative. This can be determined by the status of the essentials in your enterprise.

I owned one business which was much like Lee's army. I was so short of resources that I had no choice but to be aggressive—it was my only long term hope for survival. When I came to my Gettysburg, the chance for total victory, I too had a "Longstreet"—my comptroller. He begged me to be conservative but I had won so many victories against great odds I had begun to think that I could not lose. This is the Titanic syndrome and it may not be curable until you've had at least one good ship sink from under you. Victories can make you feel so invincible that you sail recklessly into the most treacherous of waters.

On the other hand, you may never truly know how to win until you've failed. The wisest and most effective leaders have usually tasted many devastating defeats. An amazing number of America's most successful business leaders have been through at least one bankruptcy. Unfortunately, for American business we tend to shoot our wounded so that some of those who could be the very best leaders never get a second chance. Those who have never tasted losing may be the most dangerous of all. Remember Captain Edward J. Smith; he had never made a maritime mistake. Because of that he was chosen to skipper the Titanic on her maiden voyage.

General U.S. Grant was a remarkable balance of the aggressive and conservative leadership styles. He was remarkably bold in devising strategy, but conservative in his preparation and implementation of the strategy. He did not hesitate to march on the enemy but he was wise enough to be watchful and circumspect. One of his greatest characteristics was his determination and endurance.

Lee was truly a remarkable leader, but Grant was by far the best General in the Civil War. He would have probably ended the war much sooner had he been given a free hand. He often had to fight interference from Washington as much as he did the enemy. Even so, he did not become overly frustrated by the constant meddling and changing of his orders by his superiors, but learned to respectfully go around them. The overly aggressive type will seldom have this kind of patience or humility. Like all of the truly great leaders, Grant stayed focused on the ultimate goal, which was winning the war.

THE OPPORTUNITY OF ADVERSITY

Almost anyone can lead when things are going well; it is the ability to handle a crisis that separates the true leaders from the pretenders. To most, crises are the threat of disaster, but to true leaders they are opportunities—they thrive on the intensity of the moment. But you cannot do this with clarity of mind if you are gripped with the fear of failure.

Many Southerners still like to talk about how they would have won the war had Lee not tried to invade the North. It does not take a military genius to realize this as a fallacy. Crisis is defined as the point at which it is determined if a patient is going to live or die. The Confederacy had reached precisely that point. Vicksburg was about to fall and the Confederacy would be cut in half. Resources were running dangerously low and the fighting and foraging of the two armies had destroyed the crops in most of Virginia for two years. With all of the great victories accomplished by the Confederate Army, the South was still on the verge of collapse. Conventional wisdom said they should withdraw to a few states, which they could hold. In one of the boldest and greatest decisions in military history, Lee decided it was time to attack. When it looked as if all was lost he brought the Confederacy to the very threshold of total victory.

The whole world was amazed by Lee's boldness. Several major nations were ready to recognize the Confederacy and come to their aid had he won just one battle on Union soil. Even with the heart breaking defeat at Gettysburg, Lee probably gave the Confederacy an extra year of existence. Not only had the Virginia farmers been given a badly needed growing season, the Army of Northern Virginia brought back several month's worth of supplies from foraging in the North. Sometimes a good offense is the best defense but the timid seldom see this opportunity. The greatest crisis can be our biggest opportunity if we can stay cool enough to take advantage of it. As we discussed earlier, this was the brilliance that enabled General Pershing to turn the seemingly successful German advance into an opportunity to win the war.

THE DANGER OF PROSPERITY

Just as a crisis can be an opportunity for victory, prevailing prosperity can lead to defeat. Who can count the great sports teams that have fallen to weak competitors while riding extended winning streaks? History is littered with empires that received their fatal wounds while at the height of their achievement. Success can make you vulnerable to a devastating blow when you least expect it.

If you are one of the few who cannot be satisfied until you stand at the pinnacle, you *must* go for it. You will be a drag on society and a pain to everyone around you until you do. But listen to the conservatives when they speak, and be ready to heed their advice when it is appropriate. Not only can they help you get to the top, they can help you stay there.

If you're willing to live with small victories, you will probably only have to absorb small defeats. If this is more in line with your nature, do not try to be something else or you'll perish from ulcers and heart attacks. Even so, pay attention to those who are of the aggressive nature. They may open your eyes to opportunities that can be attained even within your comfortable level of risk. They may also help you to see when you have no choice but to risk it all—those choices sometimes come even to the most conservative players.

The following are some of the general characteristics of those with the conservative temperament:

STRENGTHS:

- Plan well
- Good under pressure, seldom overreact
- Faithful to commitments
- Thoughtful
- Accomplish their goals
- Seldom surprised by circumstances
- Patient

WEAKNESSES:

- Miss opportunities
- Tend to major on minors
- Boring
- Will retreat too quickly

The Effective Middle Manager

This is usually the toughest position in any organization. Here you get most of the blame and very little of the credit. Middle management is an awkward, inhospitable position for anyone; so do not expect to feel comfortable here. No one aspires to being a middle manager as their ultimate goal—it is a stepping-stone to greater things. However, most who make it to this position remain there. The overwhelming majority of those who have come here die in this wilderness and never make it to their promised land.

When Moses led the Israelites out of Egypt with visions of their promised land, the entire first generation died in the wilderness without ever seeing that land. They died in that wilderness for the same reason most die in the wilderness of middle management—they stopped believing and started complaining. Complaining darkens the soul. Complaining does not build up—it tears down. Only builders go beyond the level of middle management.

Moses told Israel that they had been led into the wilderness for testing and to humble them. Middle management is meant to accomplish the same purpose. Everyone does well when everything is going right. Who will maintain composure and steadfastness in the midst of difficulties and apparent unfairness? Only the ones who have the real thing. Everyone *wants* to get to the top. Only one in a thousand want to get there greatly enough to pay the price. The wilderness of middle management separates the pretenders to the throne from the truly anointed.

While Israel was in Egypt they were promised a land flowing with milk and honey. In the place to which they were first taken there was not even any water! It was the exact opposite of what they had been promised! Middle management will usually be the exact opposite of everything that you had envisioned for your career. The cold slap in the face usually comes quickly after entering this position. Here there is pressure without relief, sacrifice without reward. It will make you bitter or it will make you better, but it *will* make you different. You will increase your resolve or you will lose your reward. Here, without determination and discipline your vision will vanish into daydreams that will never become realities.

The Lord really did have a Promised Land for Israel, and He did not want the first generation to perish in the wilderness. If you have made it to middle management you are on the course to fulfill your goals and you can get there.

THE TEST OF FAITH

As stated, it will require faith to enter your promised land. Faith is defined by *Funk & Wagnall's Standard Handbook of Synonyms, Antonyms and Prepositions* as "a union of belief and trust; it is a belief so strong that it becomes a part of one's own nature."

Faith is stronger than belief. To believe is to give intellectual assent; to have faith is to be inseparable from the object of your devotion. Belief can be changed or lost by a more persuasive argument; true faith is so much a part of the person it can only be taken by death.

Faith is usually understood in religious terms but we must under-stand—*everyone has religion.* Everyone believes in something. Faith is the substance of our very existence and identity—our faith is who we are. Everyone has faith. It is what we have our faith in that determines which religion it is (even atheism is the religion of "humanism," or the worship of mankind). The stronger the faith one has, the stronger his existence and the more impact he will have. The more positive the faith, the more constructive this impact will be.

Faith can also have a "dark side." It was Hitler's faith in his demented racism that drove him to extraordinary accomplishments that will scar humanity for generations. We must ask: What is our faith in? Is it a positive or negative faith? How strong is it?

In Christianity, this difference between *belief* and *faith* is the difference between being a truly devoted follower of Christ, and a mere pretender who has deluded himself in order to appease his conscience. That is why the great genius of Christianity, the apostle Paul stated that it was the faith that is of the *heart,* not just the mind that resulted in salvation. The popular and pervasive "believing in God," which is just believing that He exists, accomplishes little and is not the essence of true Christian *faith.* The delusion that we just need to believe in His existence hinders the pilgrim from finding the true religion of *faith in God.*

The same principle is true in every religion, and every aspect of life and enterprise. There is a wide gulf between believing in one's goals and having faith in them. That gulf separates those who succeed from those who spend their lives wandering aimlessly in the wilderness. They may cover much ground but they are going in circles and not really getting anywhere.

A person without faith is like a car without an engine—it may have a beautiful appearance but it will not get you anywhere. The stronger the faith, the farther and faster you will go. Mere belief is superficial and accomplishes little more than appeasing the emotions. Faith is a living power that can move the mountains that stand in the way of its accomplishment.

Moses led Israel into the wilderness in order to change their superstitions and limited belief into a rock solid faith. Your wilderness, whether it is the mire of middle management, or other circumstances which have you in a place that is the opposite of where you intended to go, can accomplish the same for you. If you respond properly to your wilderness, it will turn emotional frivolity into a force! Embrace your difficulties as opportunities and you *will* get to your promised land. Let the difficulties discourage you, and you too will perish in that place and never accomplish your goals.

THE TEST OF FREEDOM

Moses could lead Israel out of Egypt, but he could not take Egypt out of the Israelites—the difficulties of the wilderness were meant to do that. The Israelites had been slaves in Egypt, and slavery is the most base human condition. There is a security in slavery that is hard to get free from. Even though the Israelites were freed and moving toward their destiny and fulfillment, when they encountered difficulties, most of them began looking back on the terrible oppression of slavery by wanting to go back and feeling that they had been better off in Egypt!

This is the dividing line that separates those who go on to victory from those who go back to their doom—no one will attain his goal or destiny until he becomes *free*. The free man would rather perish in the wilderness trying to get free than to go back to slavery. Until we make the decision that we will not go back, regardless of how bad it gets, we will not go forward.

The most telltale symptom of surrender to slavery is *grumbling* and *complaining*. The one who complains has lost the faith, for he has already given up in his heart. The one with true faith meets even the biggest obstacles as an opportunity to win a bigger victory, and make a greater advance toward his goal. This cannot be blind optimism which is just another form of mere belief masquerading as the true faith. Optimism will wither in the heat of the desert wilderness; true faith becomes stronger and more determined as the heat is turned up.

Faith can move mountains and it will move every one that stands in its way. True faith makes the road; it does not follow one. That is why true faith is true freedom; *no* shackle can be put on it. True faith is the ability to seize the vision of one's destiny with such a grip that it cannot be taken away until it is fulfilled. True faith moves every obstacle but is moved by no obstacle. True faith *will* get to the Promised Land.

The first three days the Israelites were in the wilderness, they did not even have water. Then the first well they were led to was bitter! This was unquestionably a trial. They did not understand that God intended to turn the bitter waters into sweet as an object lesson. Their first response to the disappointment was doubt and complaining, and by that the destroyer was released among them.

Anyone who has been truly thirsty can identify with the Israelites. Real thirst arouses our basic instincts of survival. They may have had a real excuse to complain but this most difficult test was also their greatest opportunity. It is the real test that brings out real faith. True faith is internal, not external and it is not dependent on external circumstances. *True faith does not change with disappointments; it becomes even stronger. True faith will always turn the bitter waters of disappointment into the sweet waters of greater opportunity.* When disappointment results in complaining, the destroyer of our faith has been released and our vision will soon perish.

The wilderness, whether it is middle management, the middle class, or middle age, is meant to bring out the best, or the worst in you. You are the one who determines which it will be.

CHAPTER EIGHTEEN

MARKETING

You can have a great Product, quality Administration, perfect Timing and good Resources, but if you are weak in Marketing it can be your doom. Some of the world's best Products offered at exceptional values have failed because of weak Marketing.

In this study we define Marketing as both Promotions and Distribution because they are essentially linked. This chapter is an overview of some general principles that true and lasting success depends upon in this area.

STRATEGIC RESEARCH

Effective Marketing must begin with a thorough knowledge of your market. Only then will you be able to develop a strategy for best reaching it. If you do not have this knowledge, you must develop a plan for researching it. Market research can be as important as the research you used in developing the Product.

At least part of this research should be done before developing the Product. You can have the greatest widget in the world but if only three people in the world need one, and two already have one, there is a slim chance for success. The bigger the market for your Product the greater the prospects for your success. The smaller or more competitive the market, the more skilled you will have to be in promoting it.

Time and Resources that are wisely spent researching your market can save you many times what you spend. Not only can this research help identify your market, but it may also help develop the Product, determine the quality, quantity, and price of what you produce, and give you a head start for distributing the Product when it is ready. As stated, some of this research should be done before development and production has begun, and on a regular basis afterwards because markets are continually changing.

There are many fine marketing research firms that can probably do this study for you more accurately and less expensively than you can do it. These independent studies can also be a big help in raising needed capital or other Resources for your enterprise. Every banker and investor knows that as unbiased as you may try to be in your own study, your love for the Product, or dreams of success will affect your results. A good marketing research firm is going to find out and tell you the truth, and you must know the truth about your market in order to succeed.

HITTING THE TARGET

Many a great and potentially successful Product failed to succeed simply because the Promotions targeted the *wrong market*. Had these targeted the right market with their efforts they would have probably succeeded. Let us use this book for example.

With a few exceptions, only scholars and educators are naturally attracted to thick, hardbound books. However, scholars and educators represent a very small percentage of the overall market. It has also been found that after a book reaches 150 pages in length it will lose approximately one percent of its potential readers for every two pages added. Therefore, a book of 250 pages will have lost about 50 percent of the potential readers of a 150-page book.

Those who like thin books are on both ends of the social strata. Busy corporate executives and high achievers like thin books because they take less time to read, and time is a premium for them. Less educated people like thin books because they are less intimidating. On the other hand, scholars and educators who like thick hardbound books, usually view thinner books as having less substance, and therefore less worthy of their attention.

If your book is targeting busy corporate executives, but is 350 pages in length, you will probably only reach a small percentage of those you would have attracted with a more compact volume. There are authors who target scholars with their content, but who produce the smaller paperback books they tend to resist. Others, who produce the large hardbound volumes which scholars are attracted to, write them in a personal, popular style that most scholars do not appreciate. Those who might appreciate the style of writing do not like the size of the book! Most books would therefore be much more successful if the writer and publishers considered the audience they are trying to reach while the book is being planned.

Each chapter of this book could easily have been expanded into a complete volume of 150 pages or more, or combined into one large volume of almost 1,000 pages. However, the achievers and entrepreneurs I want to reach would not have read it. I determined to lay out the basic principles in as compact a book as possible, knowing that those who will read it will be able to expand the basic principles that I have laid out if they need to. I can also follow it up with advanced studies in subsequent volumes if it proves helpful. On the other hand, if I were targeting scholars and educators I would have gone with the thicker, hardbound version in the first place.

A visit to a quality advertising agency, or business research firm cannot only save a great deal of time and resources; it could even save you from failure. The average producer does not think like the average consumer. *You probably do not think like your customers, or potential customers.* Effective research can help you to understand their perspective so that your Product will more perfectly meet their needs or desires, which may or may not be yours.

The following are some questions you may need to answer in order to develop an effective Marketing strategy:

1. Who *needs* your product?

2. How can you most effectively communicate and educate them about your Product?

3. Should you go directly to the potential customers or through a wholesaler(s) or other middlemen?

4. If you go through a wholesaler, who should take care of the promotions, or what portion of them?

5. Are there trade publications which effectively reach your target customer?

6. What will be the best timing for your advertising?

7. Is your Product more suited to a short-term, high profile promotion strategy, or a more long-term consistent strategy?

8. What other forms of advertising would be effective for your Product?

9. Do you need your own sales force, or can you use independents?

10. What will motivate them to give top priority to promoting your Product?

11. Has there been a recent polling of your target customer base that has information you can use, or should you consider having this done?

12. Who are your competitors? What are their strengths and weaknesses? How loyal are their customers? How can you use their advertising to your benefit?

13. Can you qualify your promotions for free radio or TV public service announcements?

14. What potential customers may not *need* your Product, but could *use* it? For example: If your product is bottled mineral water, cities with poorly rated or bad tasting water may *need* your product, while others may not be quite so desperate for it even if it would be better for them.

These are just a few standard questions that will need to be answered in order to effectively promote your Product. There may be others that relate to you and your Product specifically. Factors such as the size of the enterprise, market, and the cost of developing the Product can determine how comprehensive this research needs to be.

THE ONE FOR ALL AND ALL FOR ONE TRAP

Many enterprises get started and succeed on the strength of just one customer, but these are usually living on the edge of disaster. The more diversified your customer base, the more secure your enterprise will be. Even with the best intentions on the part of your customer, things can change. A major factor here may be Timing which will be covered in a later chapter.

My aircraft charter company multiplied in size mostly on the strength of just one customer—General Motors. When they had a 15 percent cut back in production, we had an 85 percent cutback. Even their top management did not know how long this slowdown would last, and they warned me not to put all of my eggs in their basket, but

I decided to maintain my pilot staff and ground crews knowing that just two weeks of GM's business would overcome two months of losses from my over staffing. It was a gamble motivated out of my desire to keep the GM business which I knew I could only do if I were ready when they needed me.

The slowdown lasted for months beyond anyone's expectations, and it soon had my little company on the ropes. At the last minute we went out and found more business, which seemed to have saved us. But we were so weakened that when it was determined we owed a vendor $20,000 that we had projected they would owe us, that little $40,000 swing sunk the ship. There had been single *days* when we had made more than $40,000, but at that critical time because of the way it came, it threw us into insolvency.

With 20/20 hindsight wisdom, I now know that management decisions should always be founded upon circumstances as they are and not as you expect, or hope for them to be. This is not to say that projections and studies, or even hope, should not influence decisions, but they should rarely be the *foundation* for such decisions.

JUST THE FACTS PLEASE

Your Marketing division will almost always see things with more optimism than the ultimate reality justifies. You want them to be optimistic because that is the motivation that keeps them producing. Usually the optimism of a sales force is honest; they convey things the way they really see them, but they do tend to see through "rose colored glasses."

If their faith has been combined with patient endurance, they may actually impose their faith upon reality and make it happen as they see it. In this way they can make their optimism become reality. This combination of faith and patience is rare—but needed. It is built upon the resolve to overcome difficulties and turn failures into opportunities. However, true faith is an accurate appraisal of the way things are combined with vision and hope for the way things can be. Combining the ability to face present realities as they are with the faith to see the possibilities is fundamental to building a successful Marketing team. Hype may get short-term results but will almost always result in ultimate decline or failure.

Good accountants will usually be overly conservative just as good salesmen will be overly optimistic. A good manager will listen to both of them, but not let either of them dictate policy. Both of these should have input into Marketing efforts. If you are a one-man show, think about how much advertising could help you grow and then look at your checkbook before deciding how much to spend. Usually your best choice will be found somewhere between these two extremes of thought you just exercised.

THE BEST PROMOTIONS

Your success can depend upon how effectively you get the word out about your Product. There are many options available for doing this, but you must determine what will be the most effective and appropriate. Somehow I just would not feel comfortable with a brain surgeon who has to have a billboard to advertise his services. A really good lawyer will not have to advertise or chase ambulances. In some cases, there are Products that the best and *only* appropriate Marketing is through the recommendations of satisfied customers, reputation, and a track record of success. These will all be Products of the greatest importance and highest standards of integrity.

If this is true, then why not base the foundation of Marketing upon recommendation, reputation, and a track record? Because there are other factors in the Marketing of different Products, but it is true that a good reputation and satisfied customers should be our basic Marketing strategy. If we are unable to get recommendations or our reputation is not something we can market, that should reflect a basic need to change our Product, Administration, or even the business we are in.

ENDORSEMENTS WITH CLASS

There is a reason why endorsements are one of the most effective advertising strategies. It is the same reason why the endorsements of well-known media or sports personalities do not come cheap. Of course some do compromise their integrity to endorse products, but most will maintain a high level of integrity, if for no other reason than knowing that if it gets out that they are not true, their value as endorsers will be reduced. The endorsement of a well-known personality can be effective on television, but the endorsement of one satisfied customer to another potential customer will be a more solid foundation for continued success.

Effective Marketing comes only with good planning, just as effective Products do. You should develop a strategy for cultivating promotion from your satisfied customers. You can get statements from them that can be used in brochures and other advertisements. Ask them if you can use them as a reference for other prospects.

Even better than an endorsement may be a recommendation. A recommendation is more than just an endorsement; it is a "lead" which will almost certainly give you the attention of the potential new customer. This is something you will probably have to ask your satisfied customer to do for you but few will mind if they really are satisfied. Ask your customers if they know anyone else that can use your Product or service. Then ask them if you can say that they recommended you contact them. If you have a good enough relationship, you might even ask them if they would mind contacting the prospect on your behalf. In short, do not overlook what is potentially your most effective Marketing resource—your present customers.

There are a couple of basic rules you should follow if you are going to use endorsements or recommendations:

#1 Be sure that the one whose endorsement you are using has a good reputation. Even though someone may be a good and satisfied customer that does not mean that they are respected in their field. Some associations can *hurt* you.

#2 Never use someone else's name as an endorsement or recommendation if you have not cleared it with that person, or you may well lose an established customer.

HONOR YOUR AMBASSADORS

Another basic principle for success in Marketing is that the effectiveness of your Marketing team will be directly related to the amount of esteem and reward given to them. Salesmen are often berated professionals and are often the butt of jokes even by their own companies. However, they may be the most important reason for the success or the failure of their company.

Your salesman is your *ambassador*. Only the most foolish and backward governments will send out ambassadors who they do not esteem or respect. Just as an ambassador will speak for his government, your salesman will speak for your company. He *is* your company to those he meets on your behalf. He *is* the impression that potential customers will have of *you*.

THE ESSENTIAL SKILL

Relating to other human beings may be the most difficult task we all have. From the time there were just two brothers in the world, Cain and Abel, they could not get along. The skill of meeting a new person, gaining their trust, and selling them a Product is not an easy task. The sales positions in your enterprise should be held in the highest esteem if you want ambassadors of the highest quality.

Esteem is usually measured by the attention given by the boss. If the boss is a true leader he will naturally give most of his time to those who are most important. Attention can be more effective in motivating your sales force than even raises or commissions. Good salesmen are usually paid well; they do not need money as much as they need respect. Give it to them and they will pay you back many times.

It is also more important for a salesman to believe in the Product than to just have a good personality. Knowledge of the Product is essential if one is to really believe in it. The more knowledge a salesperson has of the Product, the more confident they will be in promoting it. Knowledge is a most important tool for the true Marketing professional. The investment you make in the education of your Marketing team will usually pay great dividends.

THE RIGHT START

Proper dress is also essential for Marketing professionals. The first impression your prospect will have of you will probably be your clothes. If you are Marketing your Product to professionals or successful businessmen, they will almost certainly judge you by your overall appearance. Conservative dress is almost always appropriate. You will seldom offend someone by being too conservative, but you can easily offend someone by being too flashy or casual. Being overdressed is easier to compensate for than being underdressed; it is easier to loosen your tie or take off your jacket to look casual than it is to put on a tie in front of your prospect. Casual clothes may be more appropriate for selling pleasure boats or sports equipment, but being neat and conservative is always appropriate.

A course in basic manners can pay high dividends for your Marketing team. Not only do good manners almost always give a positive impression, the basic knowledge of good manners also imparts social confidence—an essential for the successful Marketing professional.

Learning to listen well is just as important as learning to speak well when it comes to professional salesmanship. Few things will turn off a busy executive or entrepreneur faster than a salesman who does not hear what they are trying to tell them. Learning to remember names or other personal details can be more than helpful—it is essential. It shows that you have listened and that you care. It also shows your prospect that if he has problems with your product, then he has a personal contact that will probably help him receive the proper service.

IBM grew to be one of the greatest companies in the world. It had the right product at the right time, and dominated its industry in the fastest growing market of its time to such a degree that every other product was measured by how it compared to IBM. However, IBM opened the door for a catastrophic slide of historic proportions, mainly because they failed to listen to their own customers. When the computer industry made a major turn, IBM missed it. For years they have been trying to get back to where they missed the turn and get back on the right road. Their competitors are now pretty far down that road and will be hard to catch, but it is also smart to never rule out such a great company.

CHARACTER TRAITS OF THE GOLDEN SALESMAN

It takes a unique person to do well in sales and promotions. There are certain general personality characteristics typical of those who are drawn to this profession. Some are strengths and some are weaknesses. Understanding these characteristics can help to accentuate the strengths, overcome the weaknesses, and help those who must relate to them to do so more effectively. Below is a listing of these characteristics. These are generalizations and all of them may not apply to every individual.

> Positive (+): *They enjoy life.* Good Marketing professionals usually have a good perspective on why they are doing this in the first place. Their intrigue with events and general interest in life is contagious, and can help pull others out of the doldrums. They tend to be friendly, and genuinely enjoy and are interested in other people. They will be quick to notice and help those in need. They can contribute greatly to morale. Even in difficult circumstances they will often crack a joke, which helps to relieve the pressure, and often helps to get a proper

perspective on the situation. Others like to be with them and they are the life of most parties. They can even make others enjoy being at work, which can have a significant impact on productivity.

Negative (-): *They are easily distracted.* They will tend to waste a lot of their time and other's by talking or playing games. Because they are so high on enjoying life, when the joy is gone, often they will be too. They can be just as quick to commit themselves to other emotions than joy. They will fall in love faster but also be quick to get a divorce. They can leave a trail of disappointed people, broken relationships, and bitter enemies. Because they run on positive emotions, they may run from problems and seldom resolve disputes that require confrontation.

Remedy: *They need to work with and have influence from those who are disciplined and deliberate in their leadership and lifestyle.* If they can remain focused, they will be your most productive people. Challenge their commitments by presenting potential problems and difficulties. Give them time to think about what they are committing to before you accept their commitment.

Positive (+): *Optimistic.* They will quickly see potential where others only see problems. They see opportunity and will initiate profitable ventures which others will not even notice.

Negative (-): *Tend to be emotional.* They are often subject to emotional burnout, or even breakdowns. Because they are often overly optimistic they are often disappointed. Because they tend not to see problems, when one finally gets their attention it is usually a greater shock to them than it would be to others. Their "downs" can be just as extreme as their "ups." This can also make them prone to addictions. They are often subject to financial problems because they can buy on impulse and over-commit themselves when they are emotionally high, but avoid paying the bills because it is such an emotional low.

Remedy: *The same as above.* They need to be teamed with someone who is disciplined and guided by rationale rather than emotion.

Positive (+): *They will have high energy.* They usually work hard and long, and will be quick to volunteer or tackle a hard task which stimulates others to do the same.

Negative (-): *They tend to leave jobs unfinished.* They are so quick to volunteer or start something that they often overload themselves with projects they cannot finish. They will be utterly sincere when they make commitments, and fully intend to carry them out, but because they tend to run on emotions, after the high emotional charge of starting something new has passed, they can lose interest and easily be diverted. Because of this they may tend to change jobs frequently. They can be subject to procrastination because they want to do so many things they cannot decide between them. They are usually fast starters but slow finishers.

Remedy: *They need a rigid system of accountability, and they must learn to say "NO."* They need strong leadership and management. Expect less than they promise so that you will not be disappointed. Make them accountable to clean up every mess they make—especially in human relations.

After reading the above one may be tempted to wonder if those of this temperament are worth the trouble. They are, and they may well become your most valuable people *if you understand them*, and learn to work with them to use their strengths and deal with their weaknesses. They can propel your enterprise to heights you would never otherwise attain, but they will not be able to keep you there.

The Bible is without equal in illuminating human character and disposition. The apostle Peter is one of the great character sketches of those with the temperaments that are drawn to the Marketing profession. Peter was the first to proclaim the good news of the Christ but he was also the first to desert when discouraging circumstances arose.

Peter did not desert because of cowardice; the very night before he denied Jesus he had charged an entire Roman cohort *by himself.* A Roman cohort was eight hundred men! These personality types are prone to discouragement but not cowardice.

It was Peter who walked on the water, but he also sank once he got out there. They are often encouraged too quickly and discouraged too quickly, but they are also restored quickly. Just a few weeks after his greatest failure, Peter preached his greatest sermon. He had been given the keys to open the door because he would use them. Give them a job and these will not fail you in getting off to a good start. Peter could start the church but Paul was needed to establish it and give it endurance. This personality type can be a great leader, but a poor manager. Do not expect more of them than you should and your typical Marketing professionals will be some of your most valuable people.

DISTRIBUTION

The most effective Promotions can be completely undone by a poor distribution system. The excitement of a new Product disappears quickly if it is too difficult to acquire. Modernization has afflicted the world with an addiction to convenience. A major portion of the success of any enterprise will be determined by how convenient it is to acquire the Product. Your distribution system needs to be as well planned and executed as your promotions.

I link promotions and distribution because of how directly they will impact each other. Who will your Product appeal to? If it will appeal to a wide spectrum of society you may want to do some promotional spots on a country music station and sell it through K-Mart or Wal-Mart. If your Product is likely to only appeal to the very wealthy you may want to promote it on a classical music station and distribute it through a more ritzy department or specialty store. Your promotion strategy should work in harmony with your distribution strategy.

Because of its convenience, direct mail has become an increasingly popular method of distribution. When a consumer computes the value of his time, the cost of shipping is usually less than the cost of shopping. However, stocking your Product in a store is one method of promoting it; every time someone walks by and sees it, your Product has been promoted. If you are going to distribute through direct mail, you must devise other effective methods of promotion to get your potential customer's attention.

The most effective Marketing will be a blend of promotion and distribution. If you look at them together you will have a greater tendency to keep them in balance. Do not ever forget that the best promotions in the world will be undone by poor distribution. In a sense, these two are a combination of leadership (promotions), and management (distribution). You need them both, and you need them working together.

Chapter Nineteen

RESOURCES

You can have a great Product, great Administration, great Marketing, and perfect Timing, but the lack of adequate Resources can be the doom of your enterprise. Resources include capital and any other materials required for your venture.

Capital is essential to every venture. You are not going anywhere without some of it, and you are not going very far without enough of it. The lack of proper capitalization is the number one reason for business failure in America. Obviously there is plenty of capital in America but it is knowing how to access it that is the key.

We should also consider that some of the easiest ways to obtain capital for starting a business could also be the seeds for your ultimate destruction. Every business is in business to make money. However, many who are in business do not really understand money. If you are the typical entrepreneur, this is your number one problem. Regardless of what your venture is, your Resources are probably your greatest concern. In this chapter we will offer a reasonable, workable plan for changing that. If you follow it you can change this great problem into the least of your concerns, which should result in the redirection of your energies into areas that will bear more and lasting results.

THE LIFE IS IN THE BLOOD

Your capital resources are the lifeblood of your enterprise. If you are anemic in your supply of capital, all of the other essentials will be weakened by it. If this flow is restricted you will be in constant danger of a debilitating, or fatal "heart" attack upon your entire venture. If you receive a "transfusion" from a bad source it can afflict or kill you.

You must watch over the condition of your capital supply just as you would your own blood and coronary system. You should not begin the enterprise until you have an adequate supply and a workable plan to keep it flowing. Neither should your plan to keep it flowing depend on optimistic income projections. There are places to be optimistic in business, but this is not one of them.

HELPFUL PROFESSIONALS

Bankers can help you establish a plan for your enterprise, but you must understand that bankers seldom really understand business—if they did they would not be in banking, they would be in business. What bankers do understand, which is crucial to business, is how to keep the "lifeblood" of capital flowing through your venture. Do not however, allow your bankers to run your business for you.

Accountants can be a great help in laying a solid financial plan for your venture, but understand that few accountants really understand business. However, what they do understand is crucial to business. In essence, accountants can help you monitor the health, the lifeblood, of your venture. Nonetheless, you must not allow your accountants to run your business.

Likewise, few lawyers really understand business, but what they do understand can also be crucial to your venture. However, you must not allow your lawyers to run your business.

All of these professionals are like physicians—they can provide needed checkups for your business, and help you stay on the path to remaining healthy. You should listen to them—only do not allow them to run your life. As noted, some of these professionals may understand business, and even your business, but that will be a rarity.

If your professionals are typical, they will be conservative to the point of irritating the average entrepreneur. There is a proverb that says, "The blows of a friend are better than the kisses of an enemy." Most of your meetings with your banker or accountant will end up being a blow to your plans and your ego but they are the blows of a genuine friend that may well save you from the fatal blows of defeat.

Chances are, you probably would not even be the leader of your enterprise if you were as conservative as these professionals tend to be, and you will probably not be very successful if you are overly conservative. Great advance is seldom made by any enterprise without first stepping out into the deep waters of *risk.* You must not let your professional counselors keep you from going where you must go in order to advance. But if you listen to them, they will at least help keep you aware of the traps and dangers of which you may not otherwise be aware. In order to sail in those waters, you need to know about the dangers.

COMMON MISTAKES

It is not possible to do a comprehensive study of capitalization in this one chapter, but highlighted are a few of the more common mistakes, or missed opportunities, that are made in relation to this Essential area of your venture.

The first big mistake for many is the failure to study and understand General Accounting Principles (GAP). "Accounting," means just that—the ability to *account* for your resources. If you cannot account for them, you will have hemorrhages. Just as continual bleeding will weaken any person and ultimately kill them, the failure to use proper accounting principles will do the same for your enterprise, leading to loss.

The use of GAP will lead to strengthening your entire organization. They will give you new insights into efficient management strategies and possibilities. In short, GAP can help your overall planning and organization. Using GAP keeps your hand on the pulse of your enterprise, alerting you to problems, and letting you move more quickly to take advantage of opportunities.

The remedy for this common problem is to study and understand GAP before your start your enterprise, and discipline yourself to continually increase your knowledge of them. Most entrepreneurs are concept-oriented people—visionaries, who get bored with details and try to avoid dealing with them. It requires discipline to study and keep up with the accounting but you desperately need that discipline and the knowledge derived from it.

Probably the second biggest mistake made by entrepreneurs is the dependence upon too much debt for capitalization. If you have borrowed money to capitalize at 10% interest, you must make an extra 10% profit just to pay the interest. Debt is sometimes the only alternative, but it should be considered a last alternative whenever possible unless the interest rates are extremely low.

Remedy: Idealistically you should make the ultimate goal of your enterprise to be debt free. When starting your enterprise consider other means of capitalization, such as a private stock offering, limited partnership, etc. They all have positives and negatives, but few of the negatives are as bad as debt.

If you must go into debt to start your venture, have as a primary goal to be out of debt within a specific period of time. Otherwise you will become addicted to what amounts to a very bad and costly drug habit.

To get out of debt as fast as you can is as simple as building your own reserves for emergencies, general needs and "venture capital." How can you do this? It will take intelligence, discipline, determination, and courage. The speed with which you accomplish it is not as important as the consistency, so make your time goal realistic. The following is an example of a simple brief and workable plan for getting out of debt.

> Step #1. Do not borrow any more money. Pay off existing debt. The temptation to just keep on borrowing should be considered the same as just getting one more fix. You may be able to rationalize just one more, but then you will keep on doing it. This addiction will ultimately destroy your venture.

> You may think this is just the way that almost everyone does business now, and it is true that just about all entrepreneurs have this addiction. Currently, the whole business world is in slavery to the few who had the smarts to be the suppliers, not the addicts. If you are going into business, do not subject yourself to this slavery! If you are in slavery now, get out!

> Step #2. Build your reserves. Put 1% of gross income into an emergency fund, which is not to be touched except to avoid default. After the emergency fund has enough reserves to cover your entire budget for three to six months, add this 1% to the general reserve fund.

> Put 2% of your gross income into a general reserve fund, which should not be used except for serious and defined needs. After this account has enough funds to cover all expenses for an additional six months to a year of operations, take this 3% (1% from the emergency account that is now funded) and begin building a venture

fund for taking advantage of opportunities without borrowing.

Almost any enterprise, charity, church, or family can operate on 97% of its income without even missing the 3% used to build these reserves. If you cannot do this you are living too close to the precipice of financial catastrophe. These reserves can help prevent having to borrow money on short notice which usually involves higher interest rates, and can put a deadly strain on the heart of your venture.

Step #3. Learn to live on less. Have a goal of each year putting an additional 2% into your reserves. In just five years you will have almost painlessly learned to make it on less than 90% of your income. If possible do it faster than this but *consistency over time is the key to your financial health.*

Step #4. Learn to manage your assets properly. Use the time value of money to your advantage, not to the bank's advantage. Let's take a hypothetical look at what can be done with the reserve accounts of a small enterprise that has a consistent gross income of just $100,000 per year, and uses the conservative approach of putting away just 3%, or $3,000 per year. The scale below gives the value of that small deposit at different interest rates over time. If your gross income is $200,000 you can double these numbers. If it is $1,000,000 you can multiply them by 10.

	10%	12%	14%	16%
10 years	$54,642	$62,211	$71,055	$81,405
	(Total Investment $30,000)			
15 years	$111,252	$136,221	$167,892	$208,402
	(Total Investment $45,000)			
20 years	$205,227	$272,193	$364,773	$493,509
	(Total Investment $60,000)			
30 years	$620,232	$1,088,925	$1,578,915	$2,579,802
	(Total Investment $90,000)			
40 years	$1,763,943	$3,373,062	$6,597,783	$13,141,674
	(Total Investment $120,000)			

NOTE: These figures do not compute the effect of taxes or other costs.

These numbers may seem wildly exaggerated to one who does not understand the time value of money, or the effect that just a couple of percentage points can make on the ultimate return with compounding interest. Bankers know these figures very well which is why they usually have the biggest buildings in town. Over 40 years at just 2% difference in the compounded interest rate can mean about 100% difference in the total return. The difference between 14% and 16% in this example is $6,543,891 or just at 100%.

THE SKILL OF INVESTING

Your ability to invest your resources properly will almost certainly have as much to do with your ultimate value, or net worth as your ability to make money. Most of those who are good at making money are not very good at investing it.

If you have a "CD" (Certificate of Deposit), after looking at the preceding scale you are probably wondering where you can get 16% return on your money safely. There are a number of quality, safe investment vehicles (such as some mutual funds) that average that much or better. The small amount of time that it takes to understand and begin to use such investment vehicles can ultimately pay much greater dividends on your time than you are making while managing your enterprise.

There are professional brokers and money managers who can help you, but there is no substitute for your own study and understanding of investment and money management. If you are good at making money, you probably do not have much time to manage your money, and will need the services of a broker. If you use a broker, you will still need to be able to judge between the good ones and bad ones, and there are plenty of bad ones. The time spent understanding asset management will probably pay at least as high a dividend to your ultimate net worth as the time spent actually making the money—and there is a probability that it will mean a whole lot more to your overall financial condition.

It is easy to see how discipline and consistency over a period of time can enable even a small enterprise to begin financing itself. This should be your ultimate goal. The closer you get to this, the healthier your financial position will be. Instead of paying the lenders most of your profits, they can be compounding in your own account, multiplying the ultimate fruit of your labors.

Where would the average business, church, ministry, or government be if they had instituted a simple, conservative plan of putting away reserves in order to ultimately finance their own growth? The fact is that the average church in America which has existed for more than forty years, would never have to go to the bank again to finance its growth, and could probably finance the starting of new churches and ministries. Most governments which have been in existence even longer, would almost never have to even consider borrowing, or issuing bonds, and would be in a position to give much better incentives to new industries and businesses who locate in their region.

TIME IS MONEY

If a young couple that marries at age 25 and starts immediately to fund their IRA's, putting away $4,000 per year ($2,000 each), they will have over $2,000,000 at age 65 if they get a 10% annual return on their investment. If they are a little more aggressive and get 14% they will have almost $9,000,000. If they get 16% they will have over $17,000,000, which is $15,000,000 more than they would have at a 10% return.

It should be the goal of every family to live on less than 75% of its net income. If your family makes $40,000 a year, live as if you make $30,000. Take a couple of raises and promotions without raising your standard of living for just a few years. If you have the resolve and discipline to do this, soon you will be able to leap into a much higher standard of living without staying on the thin edge of financial disaster.

The average family pays interest on loans that equal many times what they end up with in their nest eggs for retirement. With just a little planning, discipline, and restraint for a few years that can be reversed—you can have many times the amount in your savings that you have paid in interest to banks or other lenders. Again, debt must be thought of as a deadly addiction.

WISDOM WITH DEBT

Now it is true that few businesses could ever begin without some debt. If you want to play in the enterprise game, you will almost certainly have to go into debt. However, it is important to view all debt as bad, and use it only when it is absolutely necessary, understanding the biblical proverb, "The borrower becomes the lender's slave." Our goal should always be to get out of slavery just as fast as we can which means to pay off our debt and to stay out of debt.

There is some debt that may be wise to take, such as a mortgage in an area where real estate values can be expected to appreciate. Sometimes mortgage payments are close to what you would have to pay to rent comparable property, so why not be buying it? The tax advantage of writing off the interest can also be a factor in this.

However, this tax advantage should not be absolutely counted on, but be thought of as a bonus. All tax advantages can be subject to change.

Even with the tax advantages, if you buy into a real estate market that has peaked and values are now depreciating, a home mortgage can be a poor long-term investment. Of course, there are other factors in making a real estate investment, such as needing the property, or just liking it enough to be willing to lose some money on it. During certain economic conditions real estate can be a good hedge against inflation. However, it is always wise to pay off your debt as soon as possible.

The riskiest form of debt is speculation debt. If you have an investment vehicle that you consistently get a 20% return, it may be in your interest to borrow money that you only pay 8% on to put into this vehicle, as you will be making 12% on the borrowed money. Of course, the amount of debt assumed for this purpose should be balanced with the highest standard of safety and liquidity of the investment vehicle. It should also be your goal to pay off the borrowed money with the profits as soon as possible.

CONTRARY INVESTING

The basic, successful, investment strategy is to buy low and sell high. For the long-term investor this often means doing the opposite of what the crowd is doing; you have to buy what is not in favor at the time, and sell when it comes into favor and everyone else is buying. If you are buying a commodity that is cyclical, you buy when it is down, and sell when it is up.

Most newspapers list the 52-week *high* and *low* prices for stocks. Some of the most successful investors simply look for *quality* stocks that are at or near their 52-week low price, buy them and then wait until they reach their 52-week high price to sell them. Some stocks will fluctuate as much as 50% or more of their value between these highs and lows. Some will hit each high or low several times a year. If you buy low and sell high with just a 25% spread four times in a year, you will have doubled your investment. If it just happens once you will have made 25%, which is not bad by most standards.

Of course, any investing does involve risk, and usually the greater the potential return, the greater the risk. It is not wise to make any such investments with money that you cannot afford to lose. Those without patience, and the willingness to suffer "paper losses" for a while should not play this game either. You may buy a stock right at its 52-week low price but it could still be going lower than that. It is wise to study every company that you are going to invest in to look for trends that might make its prices head even lower than they have been within the last year. That is where the next investment strategy can be helpful.

DOLLAR COST AVERAGING

The investment strategy called "Dollar Cost Averaging" can be most effective if you are investing for the long term. This strategy requires investing the same amount of money in a targeted investment vehicle at regular time intervals. Let's take an exaggerated example of this in order to illustrate the effect of this simple, but relatively safe and effective strategy.

Let's pretend to invest $100 per month in a company whose stock is trading at $10 per share when we begin, but drops $1 a share per month until it has lost 90% of its value. It then stays flat for 6 months before rising just $1 a share per month until it regains just half of its original value. As the illustration below shows, what appears to be a bad loser actually results in a 142% return on your investment if you are faithful to the "Dollar Cost Averaging" strategy.

Mo.	Cost of Stock	Shares Bought	Shares Owned	Total Invested	Value of Invest.	Gain (Loss)	
1	$10	10	10	100	100	-0-	
2	9	11	21	200	190	(10)	-5%
3	8	13	34	300	272	(28)	-9%
4	7	14	48	400	336	(64)	-16%
5	6	17	65	500	390	(110)	-22%
6	5	20	85	600	425	(175)	-29%
7	4	25	110	700	440	(260)	-37%
8	3	33	143	800	429	(371)	-46%
9	2	50	193	900	386	(514)	-57%
10	1	100	293	1,000	293	(707)	-70%
11	1	100	393	1,100	393	(707)	-64%
12	1	100	493	1,200	493	(707)	-59%
13	1	100	593	1,300	593	(707)	-54%
14	1	100	693	1,400	693	(707)	-51%
15	1	100	793	1,500	793	(707)	-47%
16	2	50	843	1,600	1,686	86	+ 5%
17	3	33	876	1,700	2,628	928	+54%
18	4	25	901	1,800	3,604	1,804	+100%
19	5	20	921	1,900	4,605	2,705	+142%

(Fractions and cents are rounded off.)

This is an example meant to dramatize the effect of "Dollar Cost Averaging," and it should be considered that there might never be an investment vehicle that will be this consistent in their downward or upward performance. One must also consider that there is no guarantee that an investment will ever come back.

However, for long term investments using this strategy *you want the price to fall while you are buying,* allowing you to purchase more shares or units for your money. This will result in paper losses for this time, but you really do not want the price to start rising until you intend to sell. The key to this strategy is consistency and patience. I used months in this example, but you can change that to days, weeks, or years, as long as it is consistent and the amount of the regular investment is consistent.

With this example comes the temptation to wait for the investment vehicle to bottom out before buying shares. This is almost impossible for even the most astute investor to do. The bottom could be reached at any point along the descent and the top reached at any point in the ascent. "Dollar Cost Averaging" helps you to use the *averages* to benefit from either a descending or an ascending investment.

Obviously, to benefit from a descending investment, you must have the resolve, and the capital to stick with it until it has made a positive turn. It takes a great deal of courage to do this, and it definitely is not for everyone. It is also recommended that you only use "risk capital" with such a strategy.

WARNINGS AND OPPORTUNITIES

There are also some signs that our economy could be in serious jeopardy. Even though the United States may have the strongest and healthiest economy in the world, the entire world's economy is on shaky ground and some earthquakes are likely. In some ways wealth is like energy which is never destroyed, but just changes forms. Likewise, whenever there is a catastrophic economic collapse such as the Great Depression, wealth is not destroyed—it just changes hands. The hands that it changes to are the ones who are prepared for it. Those who will be in the position to take advantage of an economic downturn or collapse will be those who are out of debt with a strong asset base. The timing of such slides or collapses are seldom easy to predict, but there will always be corrections, and problems that cause them from time to time.

THE OTHER SIDE OF DEBT

On the other side of reducing your own debt for a more healthy capital position, is reducing the debt that is owed to you—your Accounts Receivable. Many businesses that were successful in developing a quality Product, and effectively getting it to the market, failed because they extended credit too freely and could not collect their receivables. Those who owe you are using your money as working capital. You may well have to pay the bank interest on the same amount of operating capital on which those who owe you are using to collect interest. If you are paying the bank 10% interest on a working capital loan, and could be earning 10% on that money properly invested, that is a 20% swing in your capital flow. (Remember how much just a few interest points can mean to you over time.)

The best credit policy is written on our money, "In God we trust"— *for all others cash!* Of course this policy is not always feasible. Often your best customers will insist on credit. There are many factors to be considered, but you should have as a goal to stay as close to zero in your receivables as possible. This will require planning and consistency.

POSITIVE COLLECTING

There are positive and negative incentives that you can use as effective coercion to bring in your receivables and keep them low. The positive incentives will make your customers happy; the negative ones will often make them mad but they can both work. Since you do not want to make your good customers angry, you probably want to use the positive incentives until you have to use the negative ones.

A positive incentive could be a discount for prepayment with another lesser discount for quick payment. These have proven very effective. An effective way to keep this option in the mind of your customers is to print two totals on the invoice—the lower one if paid by a certain date and the other one if paid after that date.

You can also give respect as an incentive. Send your best people who pay their bills a "Gold Credit" recognition letter for their prompt payments. Send those who are the next level down in their performance a "Silver Credit" letter, thanking them for their good standing while tactfully letting them know that there is a "Gold" rating. Let all of your customers know that you have such a rating system. This may sound too easy, but it does work. Good business people are success-oriented, competitive, and want to achieve the highest rating possible. If there is no reward or penalty, they are also smart enough to use your money for as long as they can.

NEGATIVE COLLECTING

There is a point at which you must determine that your positive incentives are not working with someone. Then you may need to become increasingly negative in your approach to recover what is owed to you. Most businesses have an automatic one and a half percent charge added to the invoice after thirty days, and for each additional thirty days the payment is late. Notations on the invoice such as "OVERDUE" can help. A phone call will often get a response.

After these methods have been used without success there are collection agencies, lawyers, credit bureaus, etc. However, the more extreme the measures you have to use to collect your receivables, the more likely you are to lose the customer. You have to decide at which point this is not a desirable customer anyway. The one who is buying the most from you is hurting you more than anyone if he is not paying you.

The credit that you are going to extend through your enterprise should be well planned, systematic and consistent. If you yield in charging the penalties, they will not be effective *and* you will also lose the respect of your customers. If the credit you are willing to extend is the main selling point to a prospective customer you probably do not need his business.

It is almost always best to let quality and value be your reasons for getting business, not credit unless you are in the credit business. There are a number of major corporations who simply require that they be given longer to pay if you want their business, and their business may well be worth it. You may need the flexibility to make special deals but overall, if you do not effectively manage your receivables, they will probably end up affecting your enterprise in many ways, none of which are good.

SUMMARY

There are many other successful, easy to understand investment strategies. If you are going to build reserves, you need to have a plan for managing them properly. If you are just putting them in the bank, you could well be losing the real value of your money to inflation, even if inflation is low.

Regardless of how good you are at producing growth for your venture, or making money, if your assets are not managed properly, you can end up with just a fraction of what you could have had. This is not meant to be a comprehensive study of asset management, but simply an encouragement for you to study it more thoroughly. The few hours you spend educating yourself about asset management will pay possibly greater dividends than anything else in the field of business and management on which you spend comparable time.

In almost every enterprise there will be timely opportunities that come your way which cannot wait for you to become strong enough financially to self-finance. In these cases debt may be a viable option for you. Even so, it may not be the only option and seldom should be considered your first option.

Most successful enterprises have been built more on shared ownership in the form of stock offerings, partnerships, etc., than on debt. Like debt, these forms of capitalization have positives and negatives. Most entrepreneurs are not wimps, they are independent thinkers, and are prone to action while others are still debating. Because of this they do not want to answer to others or share control of their business. However, are you giving up even more long-term control by going into debt?

There are ways to raise capital by selling a portion of your venture without losing control. As long as you maintain more than 50% ownership you can maintain 100% of control unless you subjugate yourself under the terms of the offering. There are other ways, but using non-voting preferred or other classes of stock would allow you to maintain control while also allowing you to raise all the capital needed, except for the greater scrutiny possibly given by the Securities and Exchange Commission. Their scrutiny is often very helpful in keeping your venture within its proper limits.

As far as answering to others, most leadership types do not like to do this, but they do *need* to do it. There are people out there whose insight, knowledge and wisdom can help you. The most successful leaders are those who know how to listen. Learning to answer to others and listen to their input, which anyone who has invested in your venture deserves to have, may prove invaluable to you. Giving an account for your actions can help you to sharpen and understand your reasons for the action, which may help you to see other possibilities, and pitfalls that you may not have seen otherwise.

If you decide that sharing ownership in your venture is the best way for you to raise capital, there are still a number of ways to do this. You should know your options before making a decision. An attorney and CPA can often give advice worth many times what you have to pay them (and that is usually quite a bit).

It could be that a partnership will be better for you than incorporating, or a private offering may be better than a public one. Who do you want to be part owners with you? One of your best options could be a plan that would encourage your customers to invest in your venture. This can be a great way to lock in their business. Of course, this can also be a two-edged sword; do you want those to have a voice in your management whose real interest is in keeping your prices low, etc.? To what degree will they have inside information? These are all factors that must be considered.

Managing your capital can mean just as much to the success of your enterprise as any other factor. If you do not control your Capitalization it will end up controlling you.

Chapter Twenty

TIMING

Timing is the last of the five essentials that we will cover but by no means the least important. Proper Timing will almost certainly determine the quality of your Product, the efficiency of your Administration, the effectiveness of your Marketing, and the strength of your Capitalization. In essence, Timing will be one of the biggest factors in determining your success or failure.

Proper Timing is the result of one's ability to balance patience with decisiveness. Patience and decisiveness are often conflicting in nature, but both require the one essential quality found in all true leaders—courage. Without courage proper Timing will be elusive. At times it will take just as much courage to wait for the proper Timing as it would to push ahead. At times it will take courage to push ahead to seize the moment, when the rest of the organization seems unprepared and is pressuring you to wait longer.

Courage is not the absence of fear; it is the ability to control fear. There are fears that are healthy. It is healthy to fear bullets when you are in a battle. The heroes, who take decisive action in battles, or other crises, usually feel just as much fear as everyone else; they simply overrule it in order to take action. A certain amount of fear may help you to better understand your situation. The right kind of fear can be useful, but the decisive leader controls his fears—he does not let the fears control him. When fear begins to control you, it will begin to distort your evaluation of the situation, often resulting in improper action and bad Timing.

A MINNOW TURNS INTO A SHARK

T. Boone Pickens is a modern example of how leadership can balance patience and decisiveness. He became a genius for using Timing to his advantage. Pickens, the CEO of tiny Mesa Petroleum, shocked the corporate world by announcing that he was going to take over a giant in the business at the time, Cities Service Corporation. Executives laughed over their cocktails as the proverbial minnow was chasing the whale. But after a few weeks they changed their tune and started calling the "minnow" a "shark!"

Cities Service tried to preempt Pickens by filing to take over Mesa, but Pickens held his course. The minnow was not able to eat the whole whale, but it got more than anyone thought it could. The "minnow" who turned "shark" then turned on the even bigger whales of Phillips and Gulf. No one was laughing now. The audacity and courage of Pickens, and a handful of couch cowboys forced the world's oil industry to restructure. This restructuring was not all positive, but it was probably essential if the industry was to survive in the fast changing world of oil politics.

To the unsophisticated, this corporate takeover game began to look like a simple strategy to buy a small percentage of stock in a company, announce a takeover which drives up the stock, then sell the stock at a big profit, which is the way many takeovers ended. However, it is not quite that simple. Pickens had "bet the house" that he could eat the whale. He could have lost Mesa, and though he came out with hundreds of millions in winnings, he could easily have lost just as much.

Pickens' victories could be compared to Colonel Travis who commanded the Alamo, persuading Santa Ana who commanded the Mexican army who had the Alamo surrounded, to surrender and not only give up Texas, but Mexico too! This could not happen without a brilliant plan—and an almost superhuman resolve under pressure to stick to that plan until "Santa Ana" started believing he was surrounded. Pickens' victories against the other oil giants could be compared to the little band at the Alamo then persuading the rulers of Spain and Italy to pay them millions or they would do the same thing to them that they had done to Santa Ana.

Boone Pickens versus the oil industry really was a modern day David with his little slingshot attacking the giant Goliath. Not only was Goliath clad in armor, he had an awesome spear, sword, and shield. David would get one good shot and he had better not hit him in the knee! The oil industry's massive wealth, army of lawyers, lobbyists, influence with judges, lawmakers, and the press stood against Pickens who seemed to have nothing more in his hand than a seemingly ridiculous little plan. When it appeared that the oil industry had never been stronger, Pickens saw a weak spot and with perfect Timing and accuracy he had the courage to throw the stone. They were never expecting such a shot!

Pickens looks brilliant now but had he been just a little bit off he would have looked equally stupid. When going for the big one, you had better be good, and your Timing had better be perfect. Being able to see the weak spot often takes brilliance; being able to take advantage of it will require courage, skill, and Timing.

THE COURAGE OF PATIENCE

As we discussed earlier, at Waterloo Napoleon pressed Wellington to his limits all day long. A dozen times it looked like all was lost for the allies but not once did the Duke panic and use his one "ace in the hole." Then, when the famous Old Guard marched to the center of the field to seal the victory for the French, with perfect Timing Colonel Colborne's regiment emerged from the cornfield to turn what looked like certain defeat into one of the most decisive victories in history.

Wellington's patience in releasing Colborne's regiment required an extraordinary courage to resist pressure in crisis after crisis until the Timing was perfect. More than a dozen times that day his army was on the verge of collapse causing him to be under the most extraordinary pressure to bring out these reinforcements, yet he resisted. He was determined not to use them just to save himself from defeat, but to consummate the victory. As he so perfectly demonstrated in this most famous of all battles—courage and patience are brothers.

Until patience is learned, your Timing in life will seldom be good. True patience is not the lack of resolve; it is the understanding and respect for Timing. This one essential will separate many winners from the losers.

When you go down a street and see a footing being dug, you know that a house or small building is soon going to be built. But when you turn down a street and see the whole block fenced off with a deep pit, and at the bottom of that pit men still driving pilings trying to find the bedrock, you know that a building of significance is going to be built there! For truly great and lasting results, we must build our enterprise or venture the same way. The more patience we have in laying a proper foundation, the more we will be able to build upon it. Patience, coupled with respect for Timing, will probably determine the degree of your success or failure. As the noted psychologist Carl Jung once said, "Hurry is not of the devil; it *is* the devil!" The devil is the enemy in Scripture, and *hurry* may well be the greatest enemy your enterprise will ever have.

THE COURAGE OF DECISIVENESS

Patience is fundamental to proper Timing, but decisiveness is no less necessary. Success is often achieved like a surfer catching a wave. In order for him to catch the wave, he must first discern where the wave is going to break and be positioned there. Then, when the right wave comes along, *he cannot hesitate*—if he does the wave will pass him by. To take advantage of opportunity, one must first discern where that opportunity is going to come and then be positioned properly. Then, when that opportunity does come he must be ready to act—few will wait for long. If you have come so far as to be in the right place at the right time, do not let hesitation kill your chance. Go for it!

SUMMARY

This is meant to be but a cursory study of the basic principles of Leadership, Management, and the Five Essentials for success in each. There is a great deal more depth to the understanding of each than could possibly be presented in this brief study.

The information provided here might be practical and useful, but my primary intention for presenting this book is to stimulate thought and further study. True leadership and quality management are a lifestyle, not just a course to breeze through. This lifestyle requires the continual sharpening of one's skills and knowledge. When that ceases, your leadership, your management, and your life will almost certainly be in retreat.

As I stated in the beginning, I do not have the academic credentials to be considered an expert on any of the subjects presented here. I merely have experience, both good and bad which I have tried to convey in an interesting format to those who are seeking meaningful success. If this book has stimulated a desire for a deeper understanding of the subject matter, then it has accomplished its purpose.

**For a free catalog
of other books
and materials
by Rick Joyner,
please call
1-800-542-0278**

www.morningstarministries.org

MorningStar
On the Internet

www.morningstarministries.org

**For other books
and materials
by MorningStar
check out
our website.**

www.morningstarministries.org

www.morningstarministries.org

www.morningstarministries.org

www.morningstarministries.org

www.morningstarministries.org

www.morningstarministries.org

www.morningstarministries.org

www.morningstarministries.org

www.morningstarministries.org

www.morningstarministries.org

www.morningstarministries.org

www.morningstarministries.org